LEARN TO COUNT TO 100!

Help kids learn to count to 100!

Each lesson increases the counting by 10 until they reach 100.

Each lesson includes opportunities to count the numbers, write the numbers, as well as a fun color by number and connect the dot.

Keep the learning going by counting out loud when you're walking/driving places or counting real objects.

Place pages in a sheet protector and have kids use a dry erase marker so that you practice multiple times.

BONUS: Includes bonus section to work on skip counting by 5's and 10's.

Love kids crafts & activities?
Visit our website to find
fun ideas & free printables!

TOTSCHOOLRESOURCES.COM

I Can Count to 10

1 2 3

4 5 6

7 8 9

10

I Can Write 1-10

  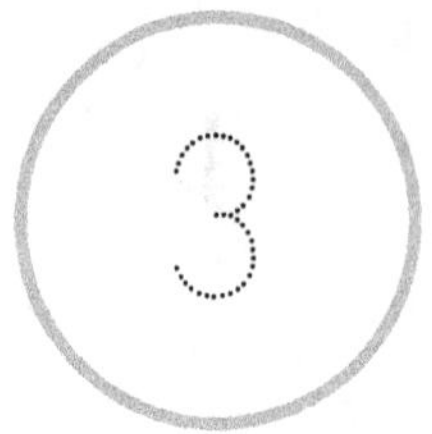

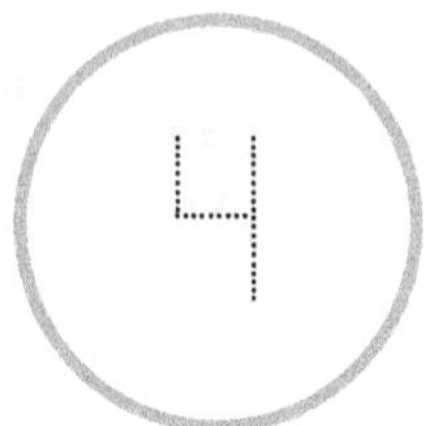 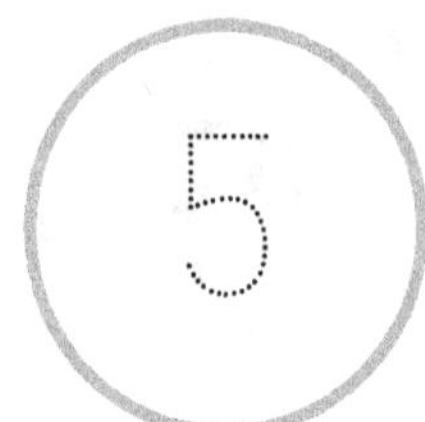 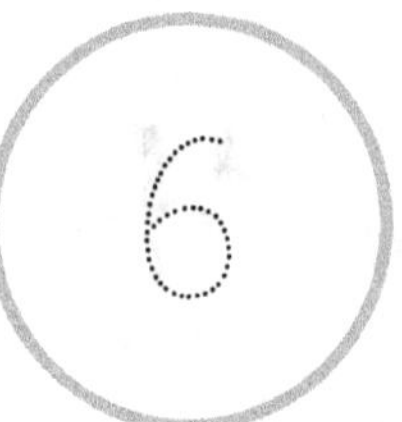

 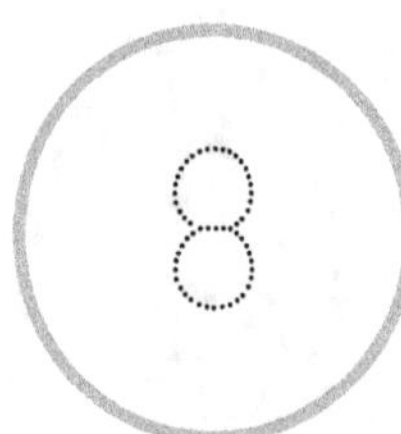 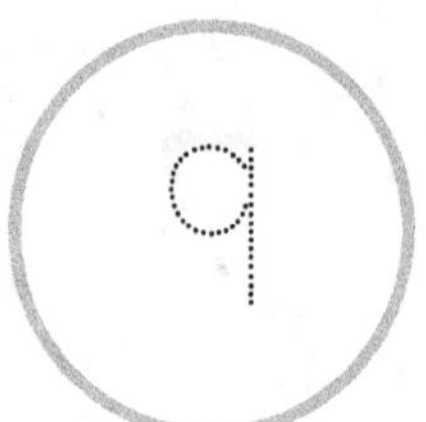

Write the missing numbers
1-10

| 1 | 2 | | 4 | 5 | 6 | 7 | | 9 | 10 |

| 1 | 2 | 3 | 4 | | 6 | 7 | 8 | | 10 |

| 1 | | 3 | 4 | 5 | 6 | | 8 | 9 | 10 |

| 1 | 2 | | 4 | 5 | | 7 | 8 | 9 | |

| | 2 | 3 | | 5 | 6 | 7 | | 9 | 10 |

Color By Number 1-9

Connect the Dots 1-10

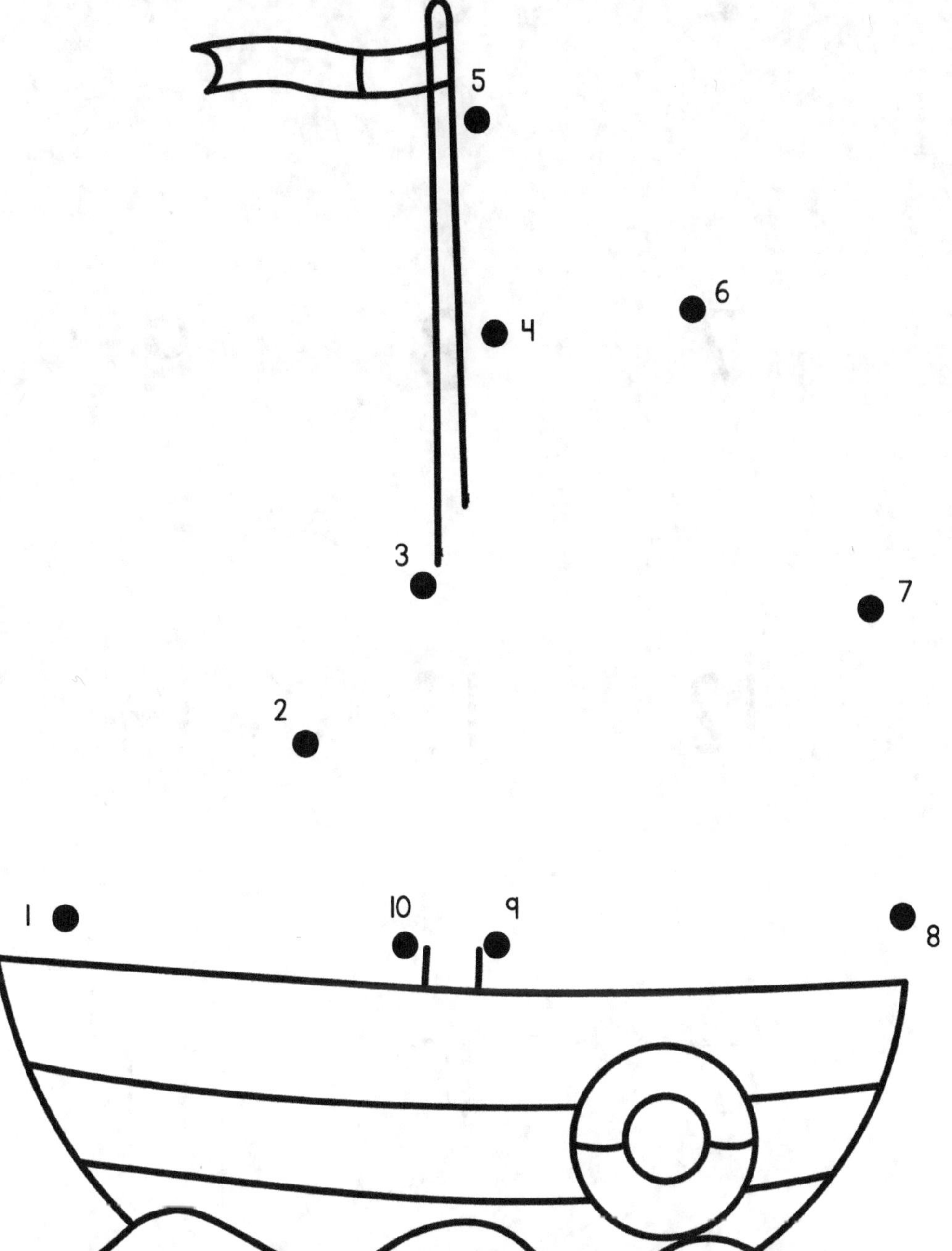

I Can Count to 20

(1) (2) (3) (4) (5)

(6) (7) (8) (9) (10)

(11) (12) (13) (14) (15)

(16) (17) (18) (19) (20)

I Can Write 1-20

Write the missing numbers 1-20

Row 1:
1 | 2 | ☐ | 4 | 5 | 6 | ☐ | 8 | 9 | 10
11 | ☐ | 13 | 14 | 15 | 16 | 17 | 18 | ☐ | 20

Row 2:
☐ | 2 | 3 | 4 | 5 | 6 | ☐ | 8 | 9 | 10
11 | 12 | 13 | ☐ | 15 | 16 | 17 | ☐ | 19 | 20

Row 3:
1 | ☐ | 3 | 4 | 5 | ☐ | 7 | 8 | 9 | ☐
11 | ☐ | 13 | 14 | ☐ | 16 | 17 | ☐ | 19 | 20

Row 4:
1 | 2 | 3 | ☐ | 5 | 6 | ☐ | 8 | ☐ | 10
☐ | 12 | ☐ | 14 | 15 | ☐ | 17 | 18 | 19 | 20

Write the missing numbers 1-20

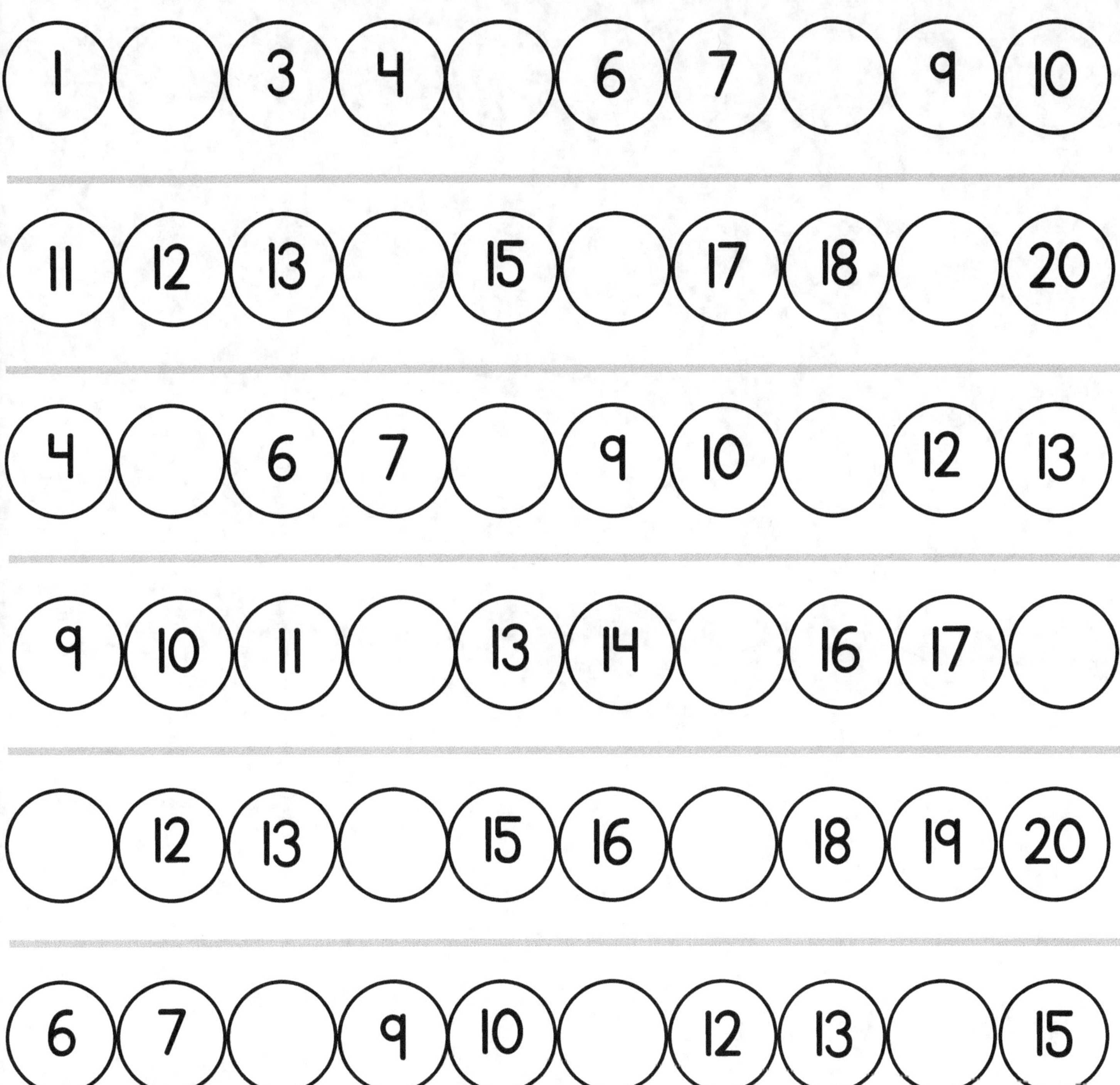

Color By Number 10-16

10 dark green
11 orange
12 brown
13 yellow
14 blue
15 purple
16 light green

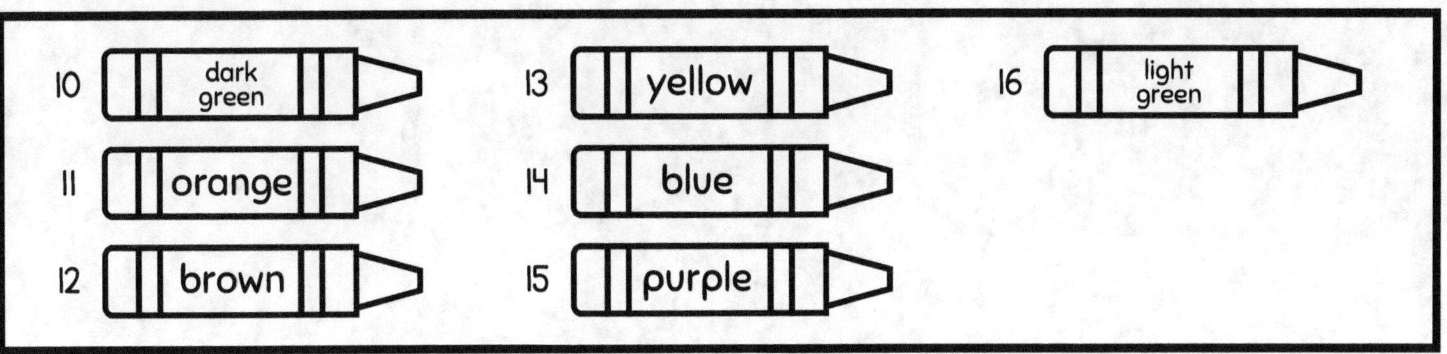

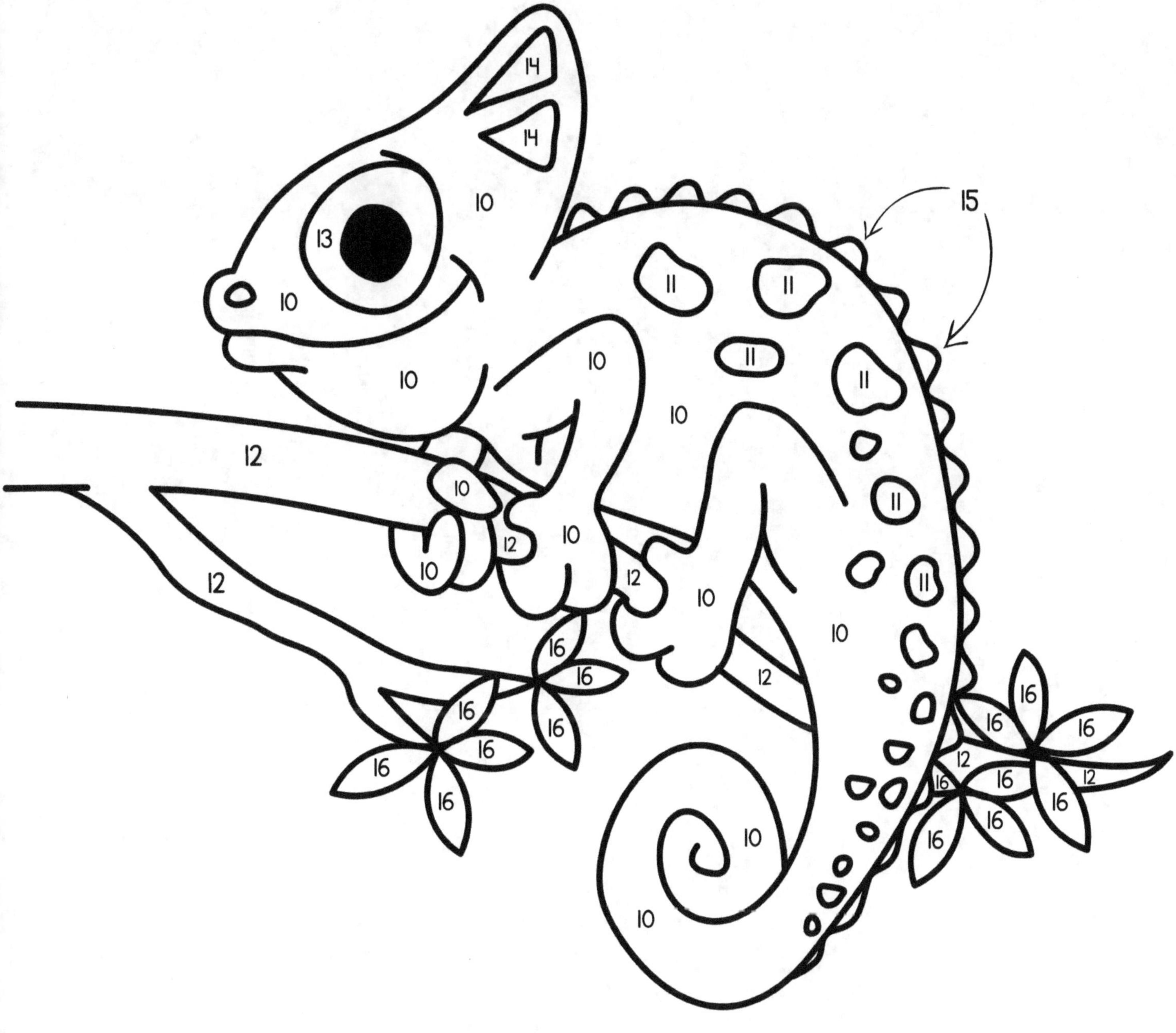

Connect the Dots 1-20

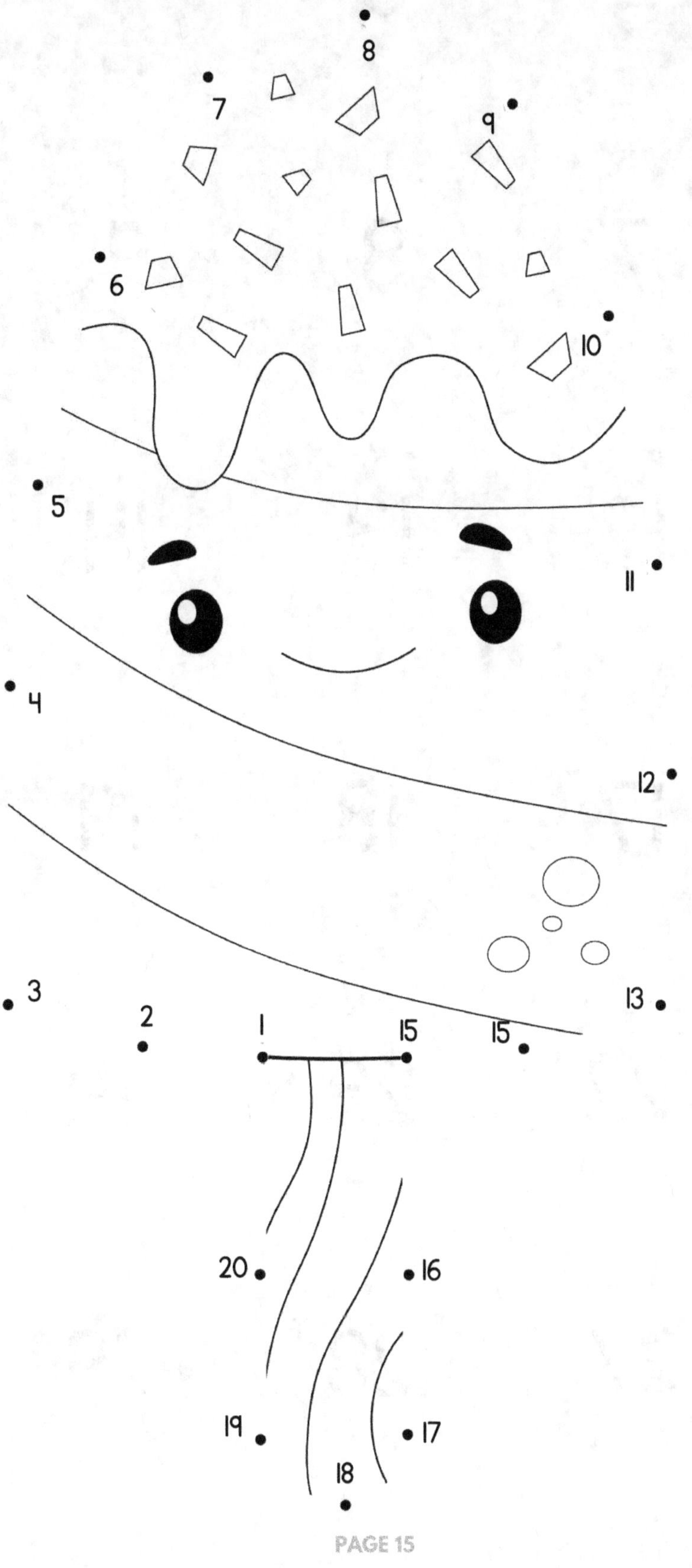

I Can Count to 30

1	2	3	4	5
6	7	8	9	10
11	12	13	14	15
16	17	18	19	20
21	22	23	24	25
26	27	28	29	30

I Can Write 1-30

Write the missing numbers 1-30

Grid 1:

1	2		4	5	6		8	9	
11		13	14	15		17	18		20
21	22		24	25		27		29	30

Grid 2:

	2	3	4		6		8	9	10
11	12		14	15	16		18	19	
21		23	24	25		27	28		30

Write the missing numbers 1-30

Write the missing numbers
1-30

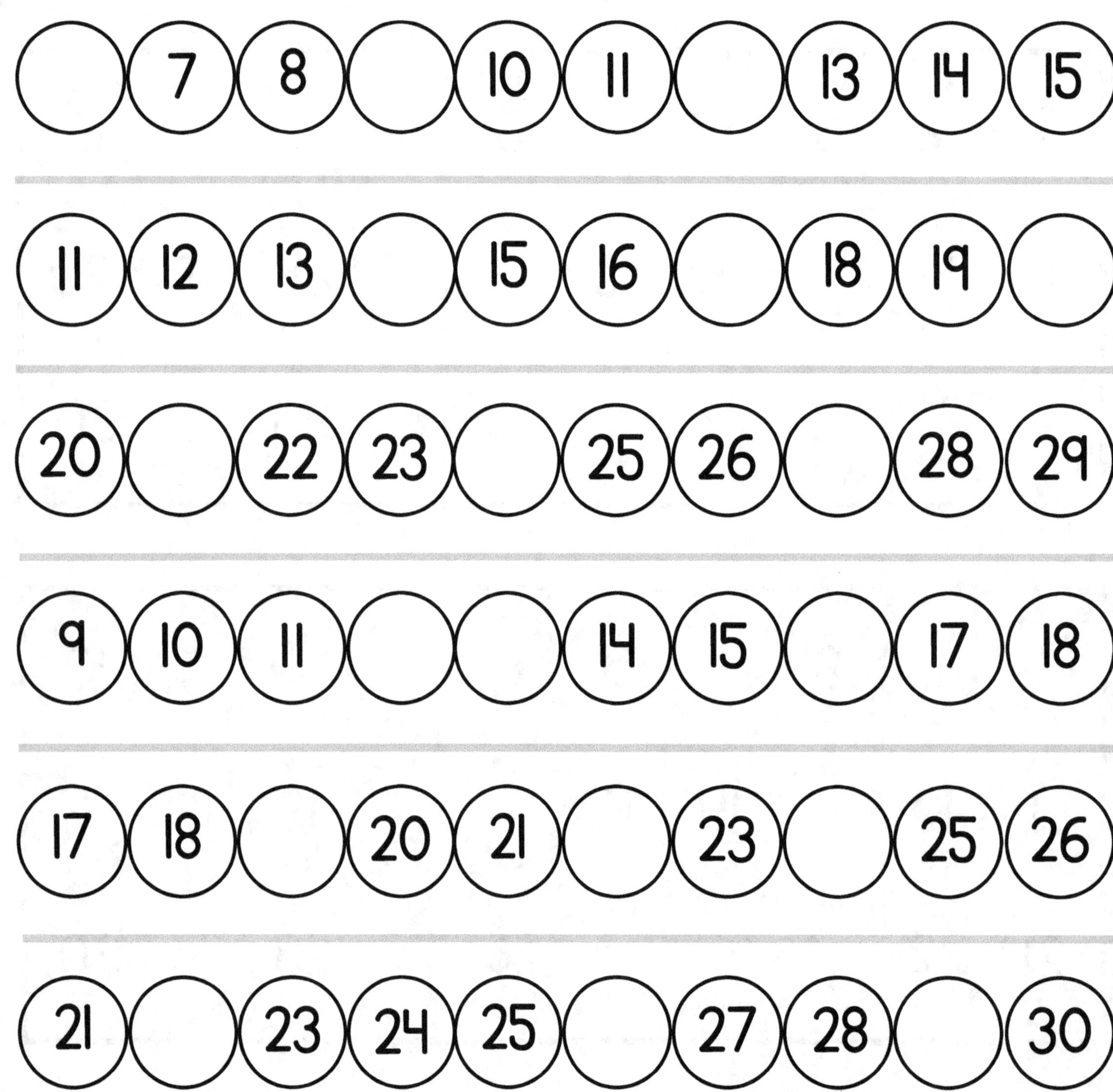

Color By Number 21-27

21	light blue	24	yellow	27	light pink
22	purple	25	blue		
23	pink	26	grey		

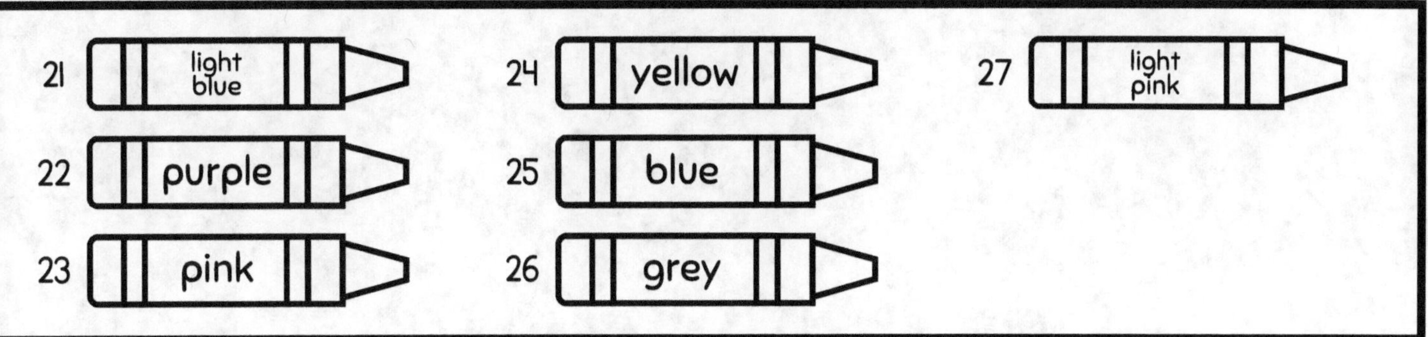

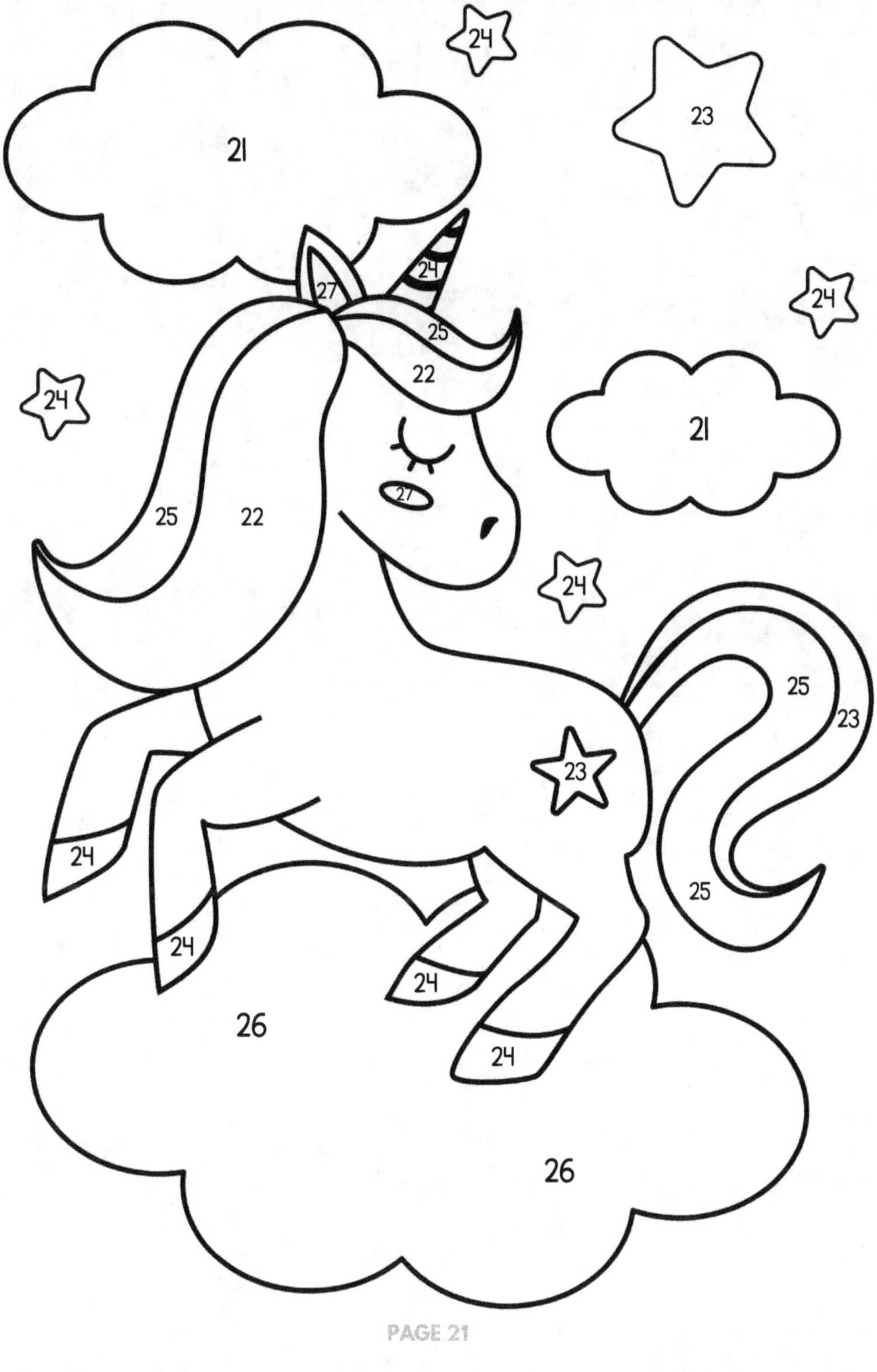

Connect the Dots 1-30

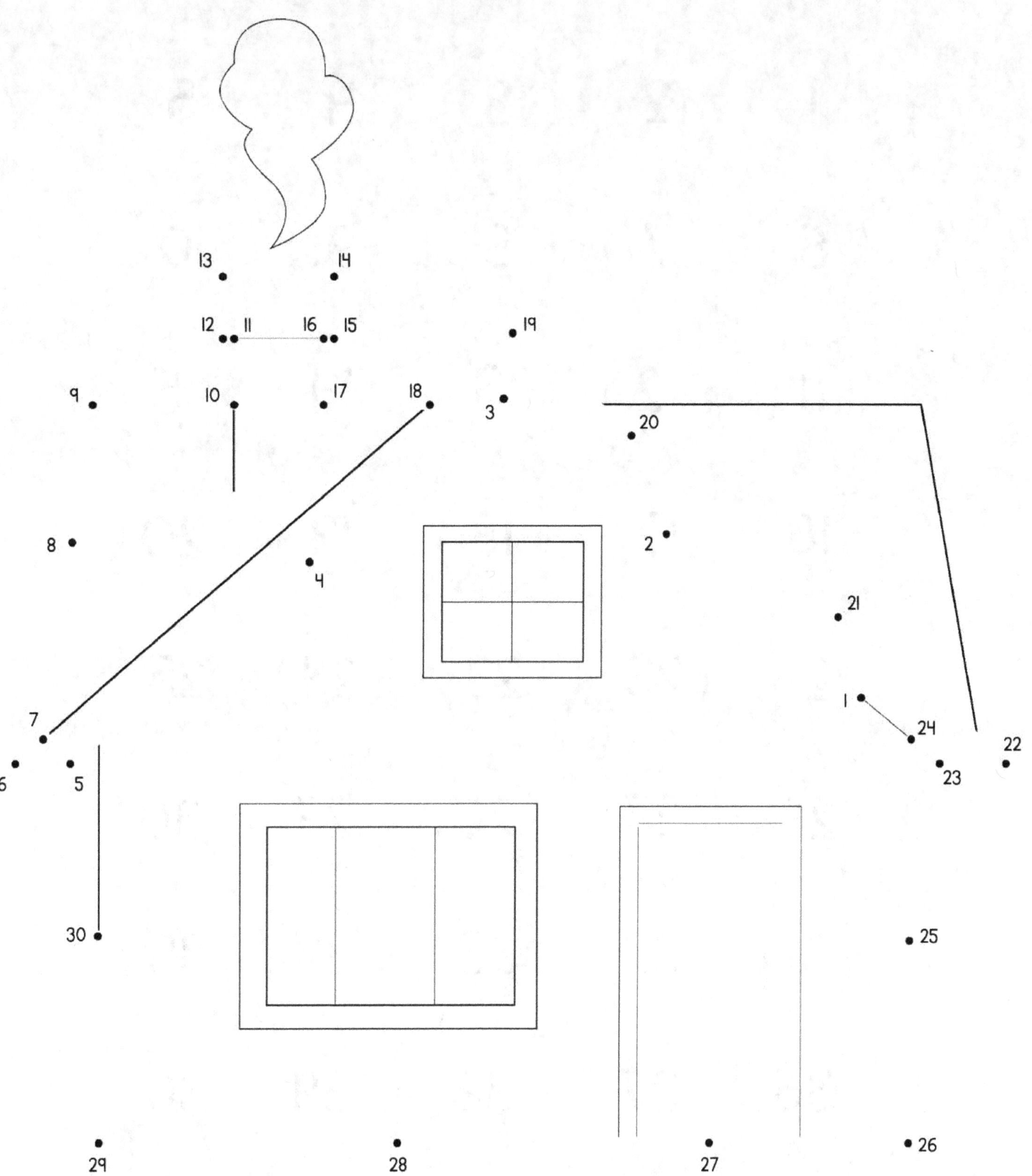

I Can Count to 40

<table>
<tr><td>1</td><td>2</td><td>3</td><td>4</td><td>5</td></tr>
<tr><td>6</td><td>7</td><td>8</td><td>9</td><td>10</td></tr>
<tr><td>11</td><td>12</td><td>13</td><td>14</td><td>15</td></tr>
<tr><td>16</td><td>17</td><td>18</td><td>19</td><td>20</td></tr>
<tr><td>21</td><td>22</td><td>23</td><td>24</td><td>25</td></tr>
<tr><td>26</td><td>27</td><td>28</td><td>29</td><td>30</td></tr>
<tr><td>31</td><td>32</td><td>33</td><td>34</td><td>35</td></tr>
<tr><td>36</td><td>37</td><td>38</td><td>39</td><td>40</td></tr>
</table>

I Can Write 1-40

Write the missing numbers
1-40

1	2	3		5	6	7		9	
11		13	14		16	17		19	20
21	22		24	25		27	28		30
	32	33	34		36		38	39	40

1		3	4	5		7	8		10
11	12	13	14	15	16	17	18	19	20
21	22	23	24	25	26	27	28	29	30
31	32	33	34	35	36	37	38	39	40

Write the missing numbers 1-40

1	2	3	4	5	6	7	8	9	10
11	12	13	14	15	16	17	18	19	20
21	22	23	24	25	26	27	28	29	30
31	32	33	34	35	36	37	38	39	40

1	2	3	4	5	6	7	8	9	10
11	12	13	14	15	16	17	18	19	20
21	22	23	24	25	26	27	28	29	30
31	32	33	34	35	36	37	38	39	40

Write the missing numbers
1-40

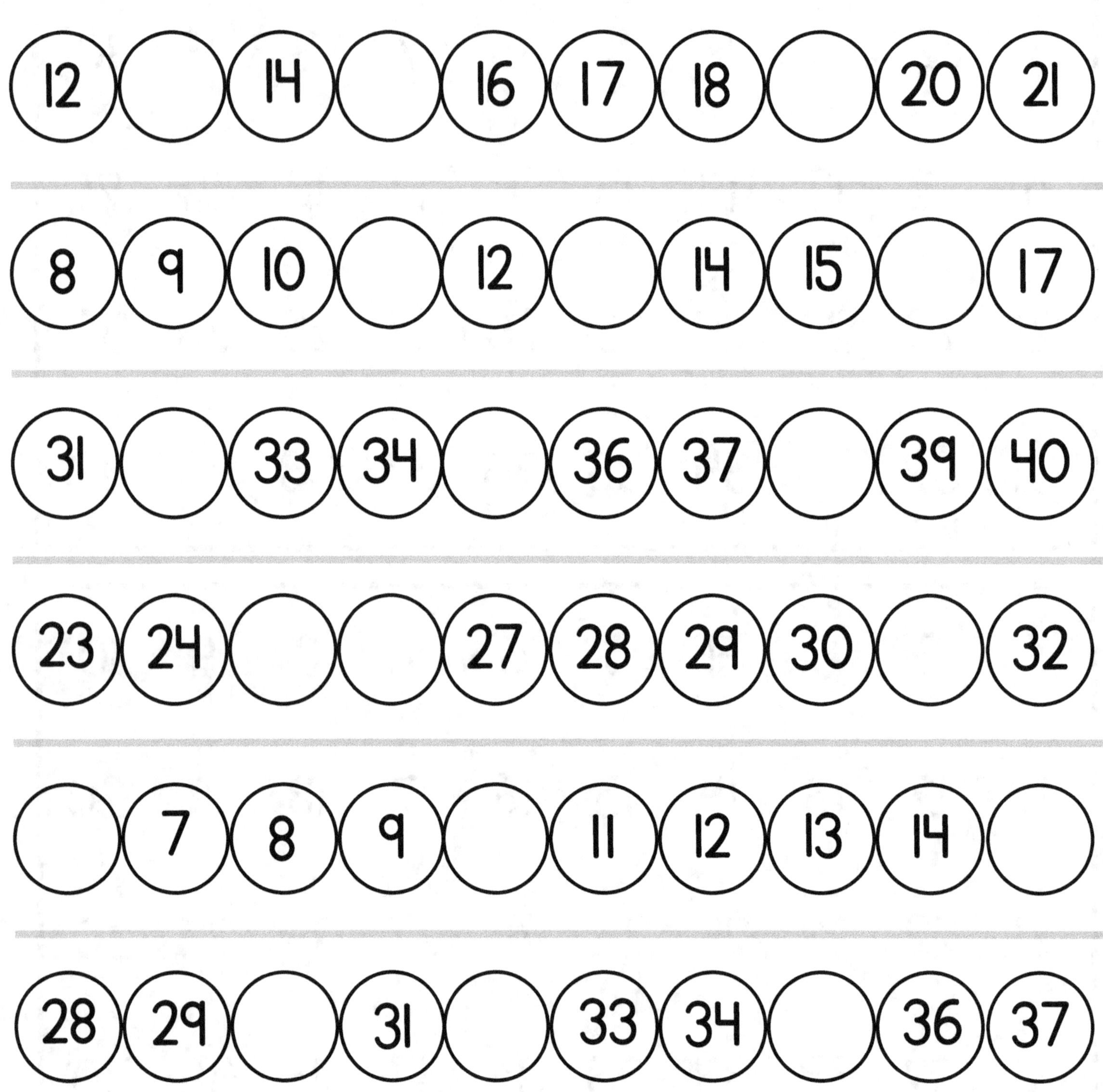

Color By Number 31-38

31 black	34 yellow	37 light green
32 orange	35 blue	38 dark green
33 pink	36 purple	

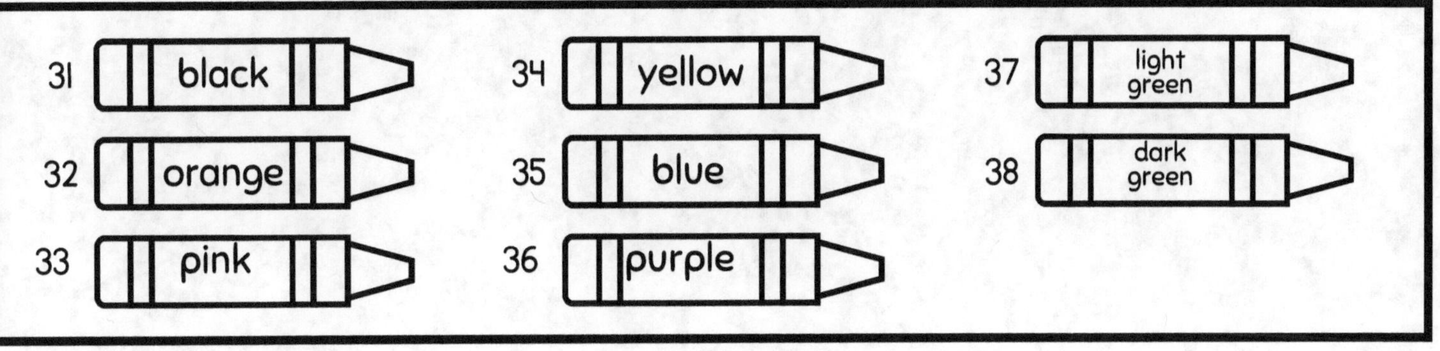

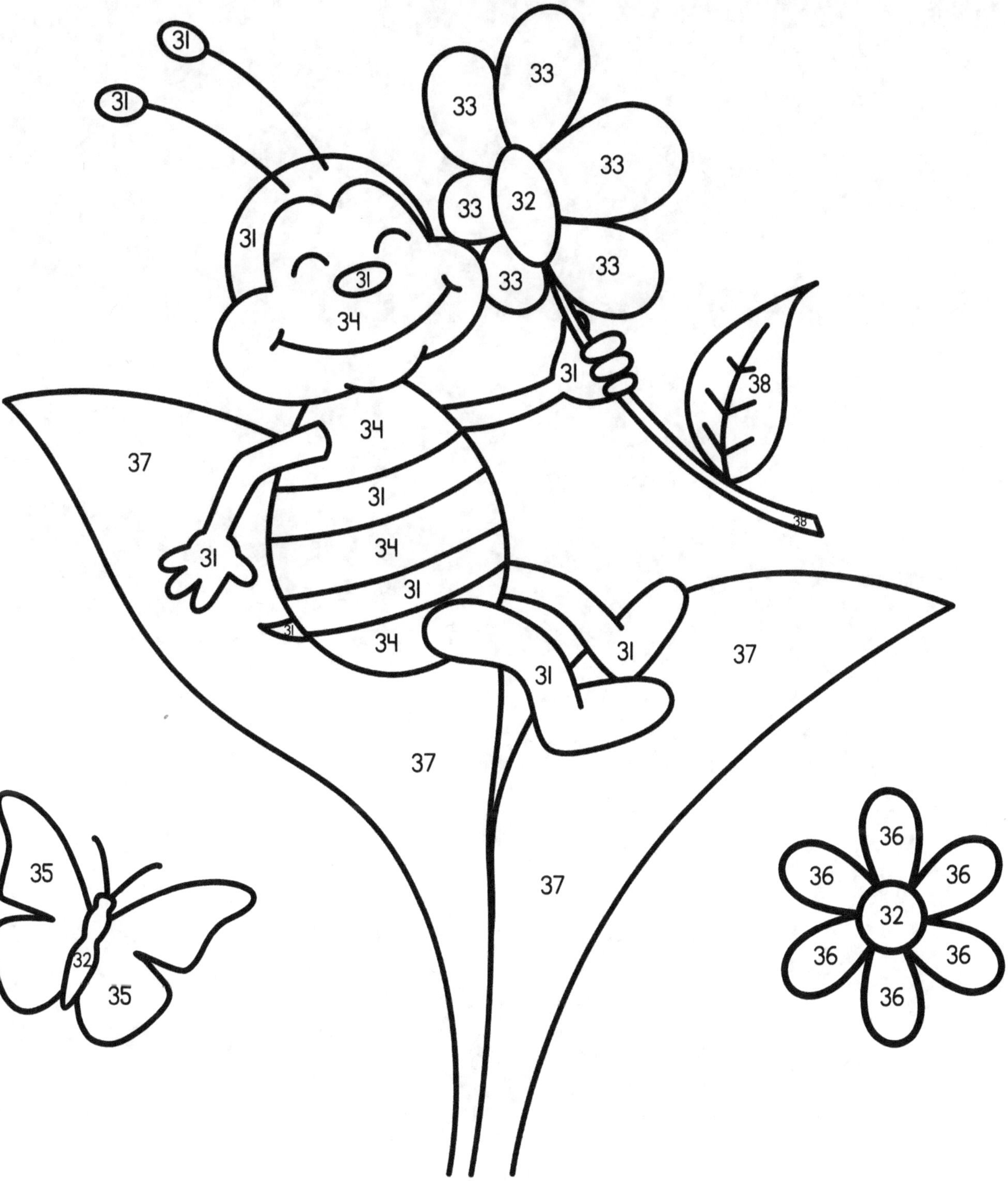

Connect the Dots 1-40

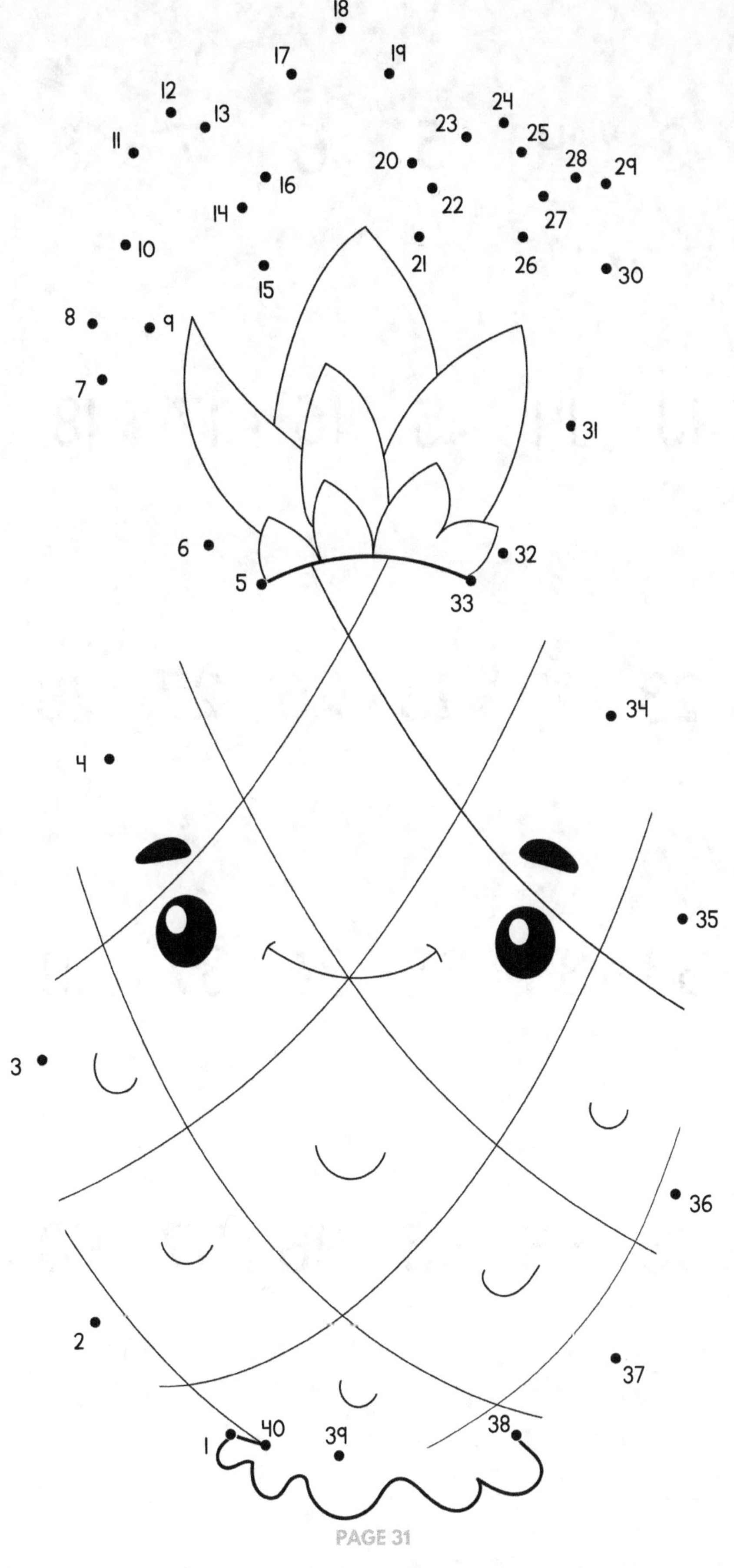

I Can Count to 50

1 2 3 4 5 6 7 8 9 10

11 12 13 14 15 16 17 18 19 20

21 22 23 24 25 26 27 28 29 30

31 32 33 34 35 36 37 38 39 40

41 42 43 44 45 46 47 48 49 50

I Can Write 1-50

1 2 3 4 5 6 7 8 9 10

11 12 13 14 15 16 17 18 19 20

21 22 23 24 25 26 27 28 29 30

31 32 33 34 35 36 37 38 39 40

41 42 43 44 45 46 47 48 49 50

Write the missing numbers
1-50

1	2	3		5		7	8		10
11		13	14		16	17		19	20
21	22		24	25	26		28	29	
31	32	33		35	36		38		40
	42	43	44		46	47		49	50

Write the missing numbers
1-50

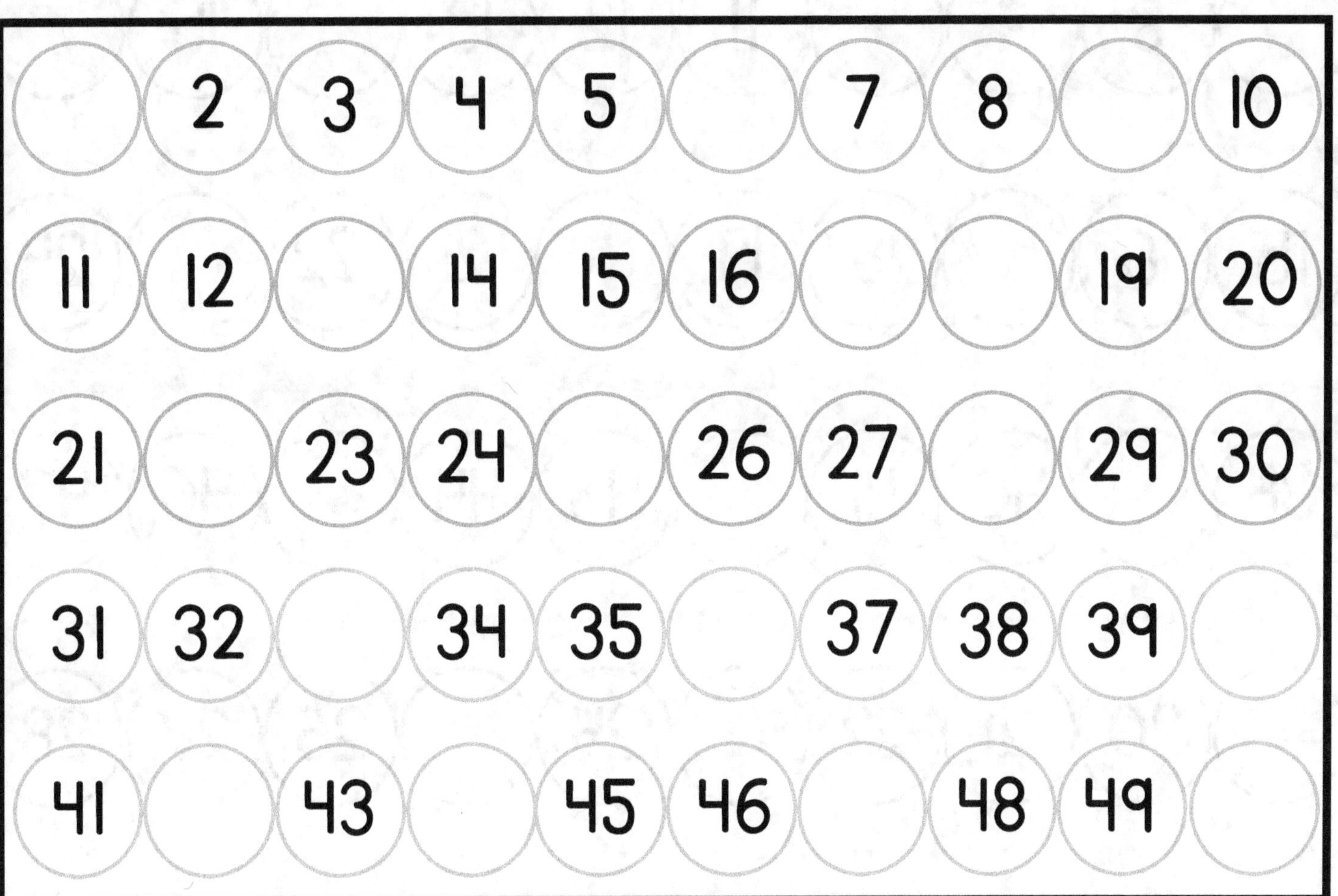

Write the missing numbers
1-50

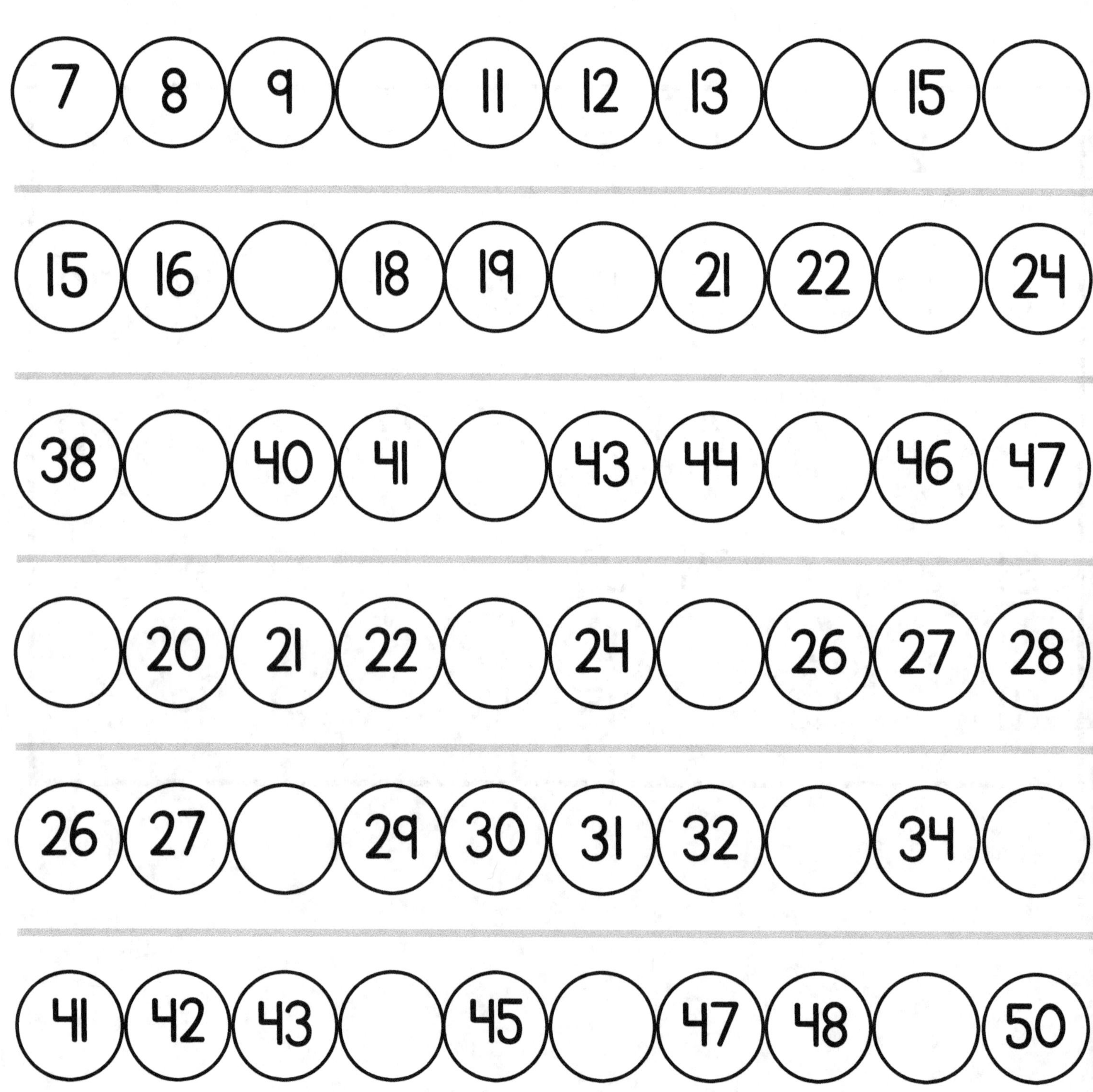

Color By Number 41-47

Connect the Dots 1-50

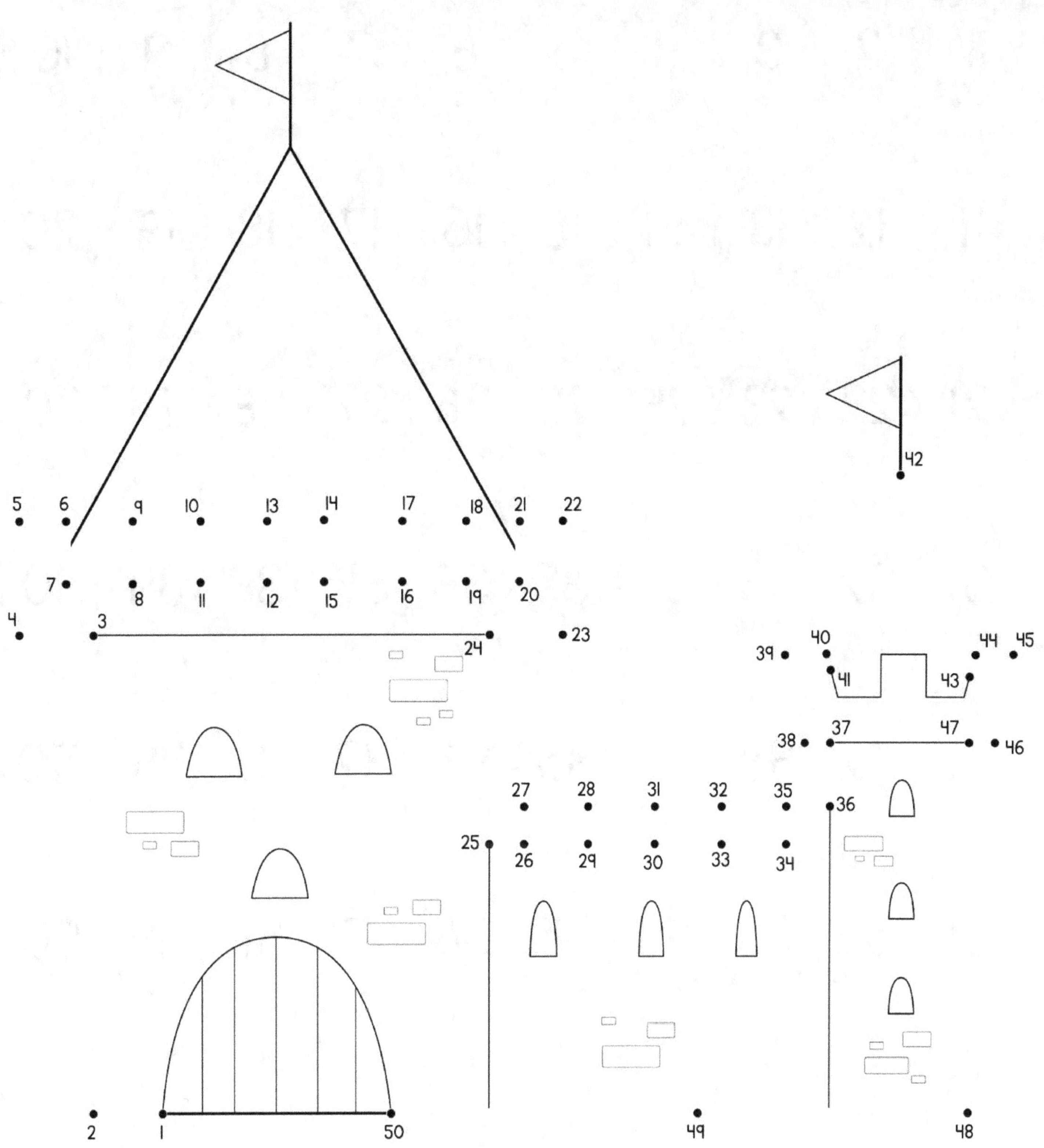

I Can Count to 60

1	2	3	4	5	6	7	8	9	10
11	12	13	14	15	16	17	18	19	20
21	22	23	24	25	26	27	28	29	30
31	32	33	34	35	36	37	38	39	40
41	42	43	44	45	46	47	48	49	50
51	52	53	54	55	56	57	58	59	60

I Can Write 1-60

1 2 3 4 5 6 7 8 9 10

11 12 13 14 15 16 17 18 19 20

21 22 23 24 25 26 27 28 29 30

31 32 33 34 35 36 37 38 39 40

41 42 43 44 45 46 47 48 49 50

51 52 53 54 55 56 57 58 59 60

Write the missing numbers
1-60

1	2	3	4		6	7			10
11	12		14	15		17		19	20
21		23		25	26	27	28		30
	32	33	34		36		38	39	40
41	42		44	45		47	48	49	
51	52		54		56	57		59	60

Write the missing numbers 1-60

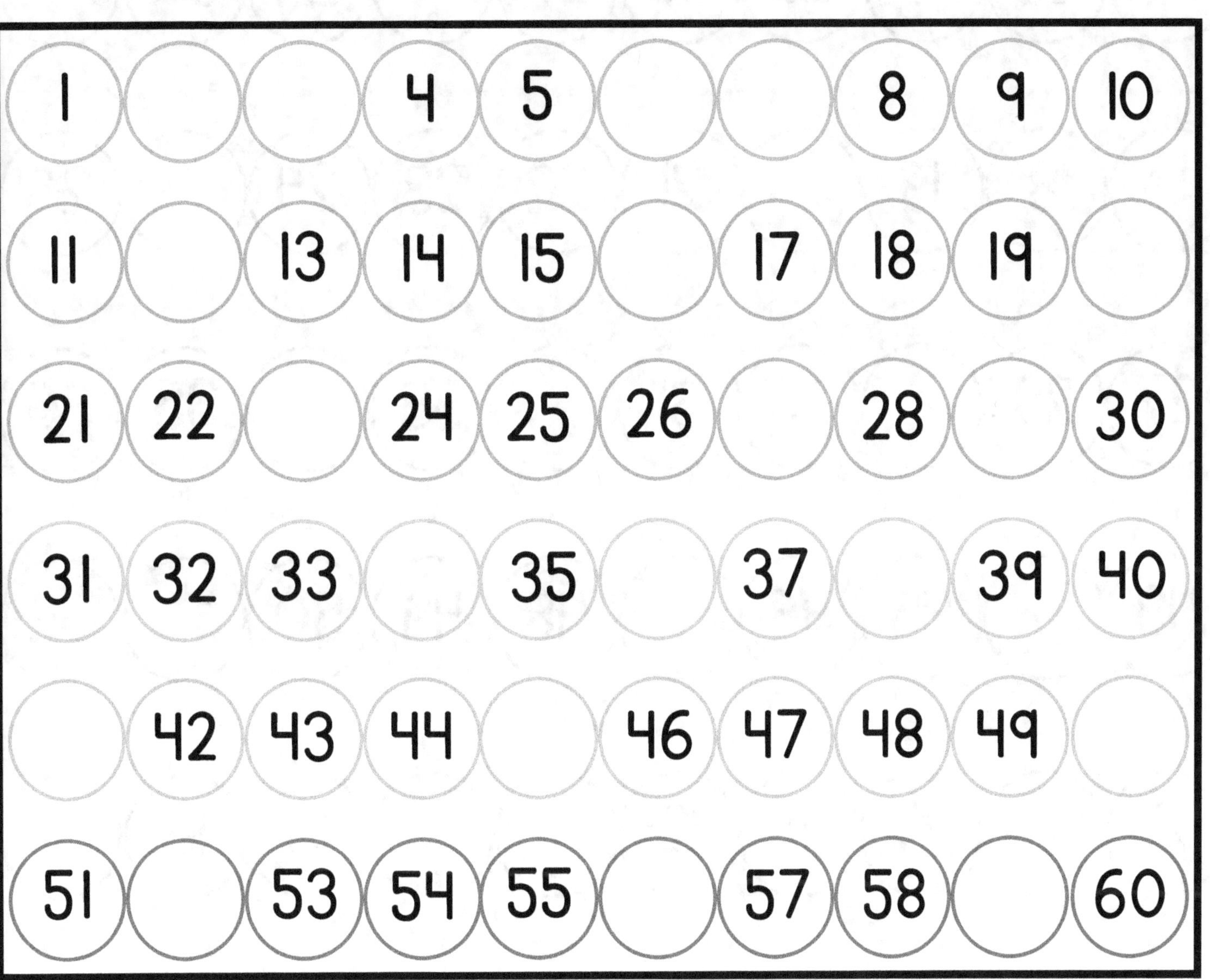

Write the missing numbers 1-60

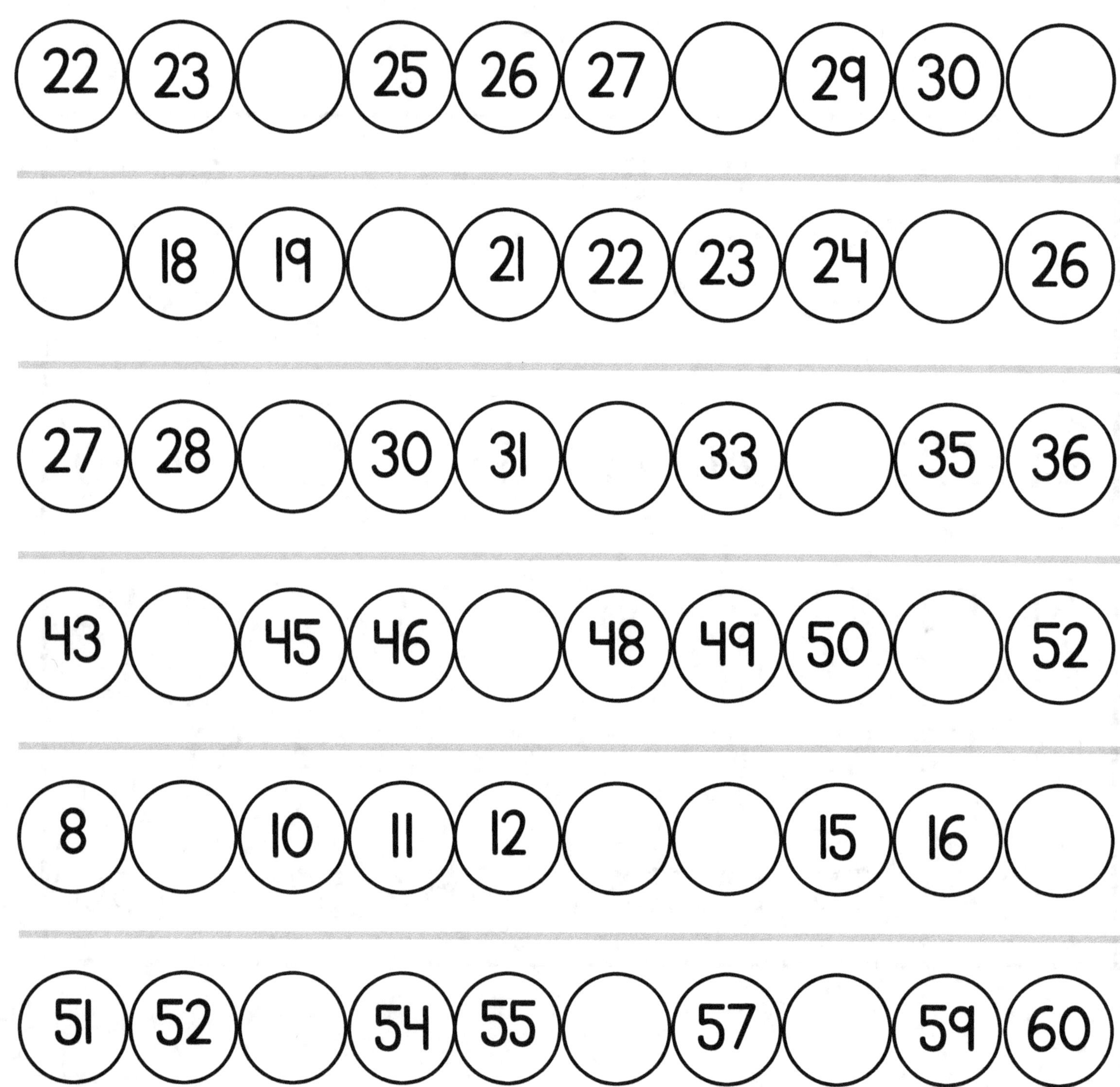

Color By Number 51-57

Connect the Dots 1-60

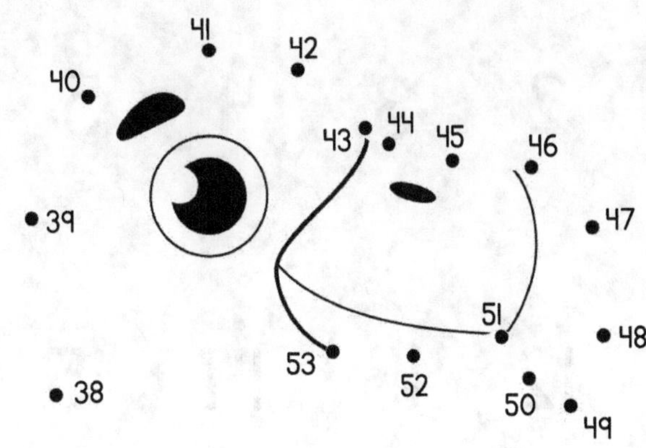

I Can Count to 70

1	2	3	4	5	6	7	8	9	10
11	12	13	14	15	16	17	18	19	20
21	22	23	24	25	26	27	28	29	30
31	32	33	34	35	36	37	38	39	40
41	42	43	44	45	46	47	48	49	50
51	52	53	54	55	56	57	58	59	60
61	62	63	64	65	66	67	68	69	70

I Can Write 1-70

1 2 3 4 5 6 7 8 9 10

11 12 13 14 15 16 17 18 19 20

21 22 23 24 25 26 27 28 29 30

31 32 33 34 35 36 37 38 39 40

41 42 43 44 45 46 47 48 49 50

51 52 53 54 55 56 57 58 59 60

61 62 63 64 65 66 67 68 69 70

Write the missing numbers 1-70

1	2		4	5		7		9	10
11	12	13		15	16		18	19	
21		23	24		26	27	28		30
31	32		34		36	37		39	40
	42	43		45	46		48	49	50
51		53	54	55		57	58	59	
61		63	64	65		67	68		70

Write the missing numbers
1-70

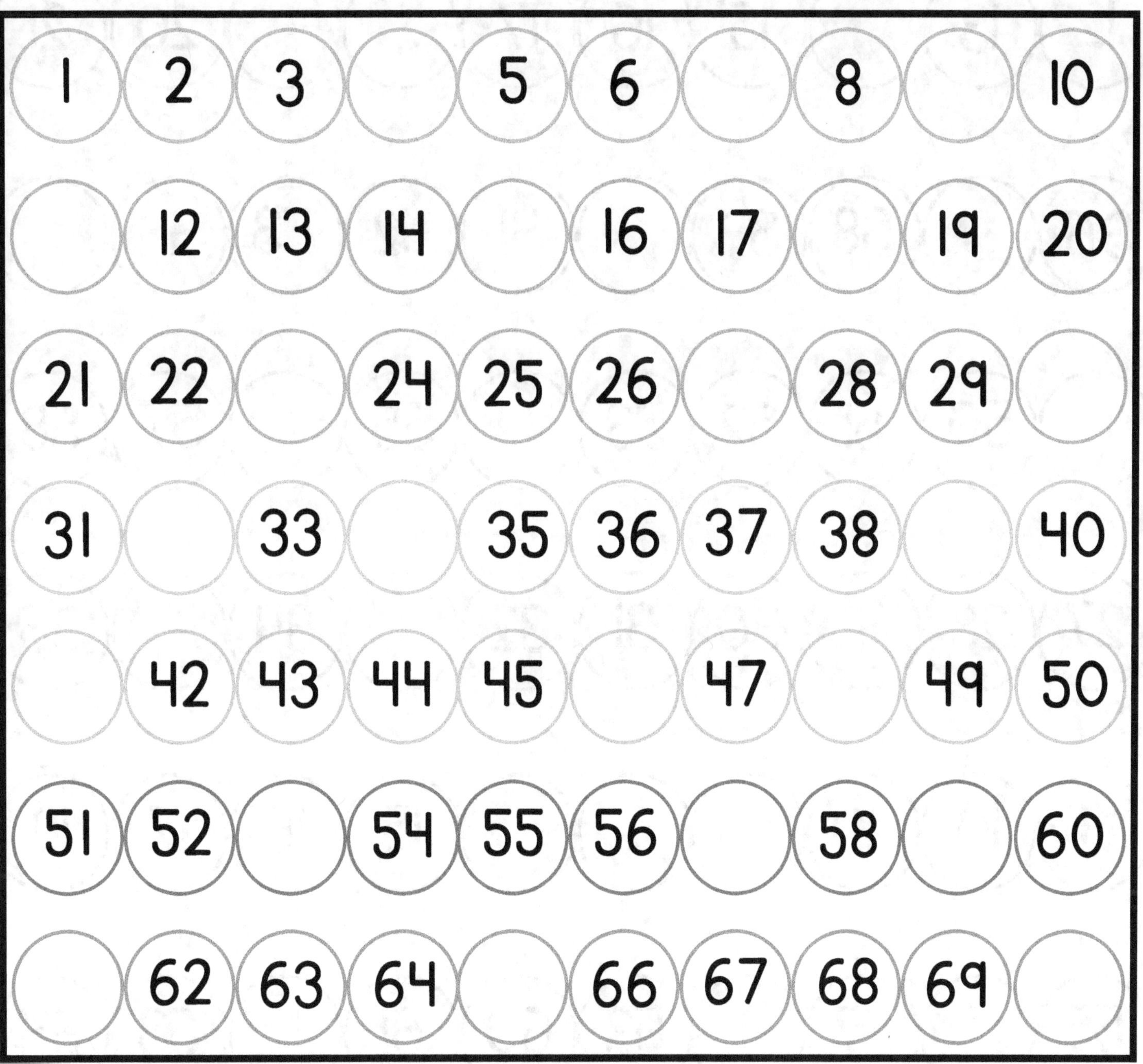

Write the missing numbers
1-70

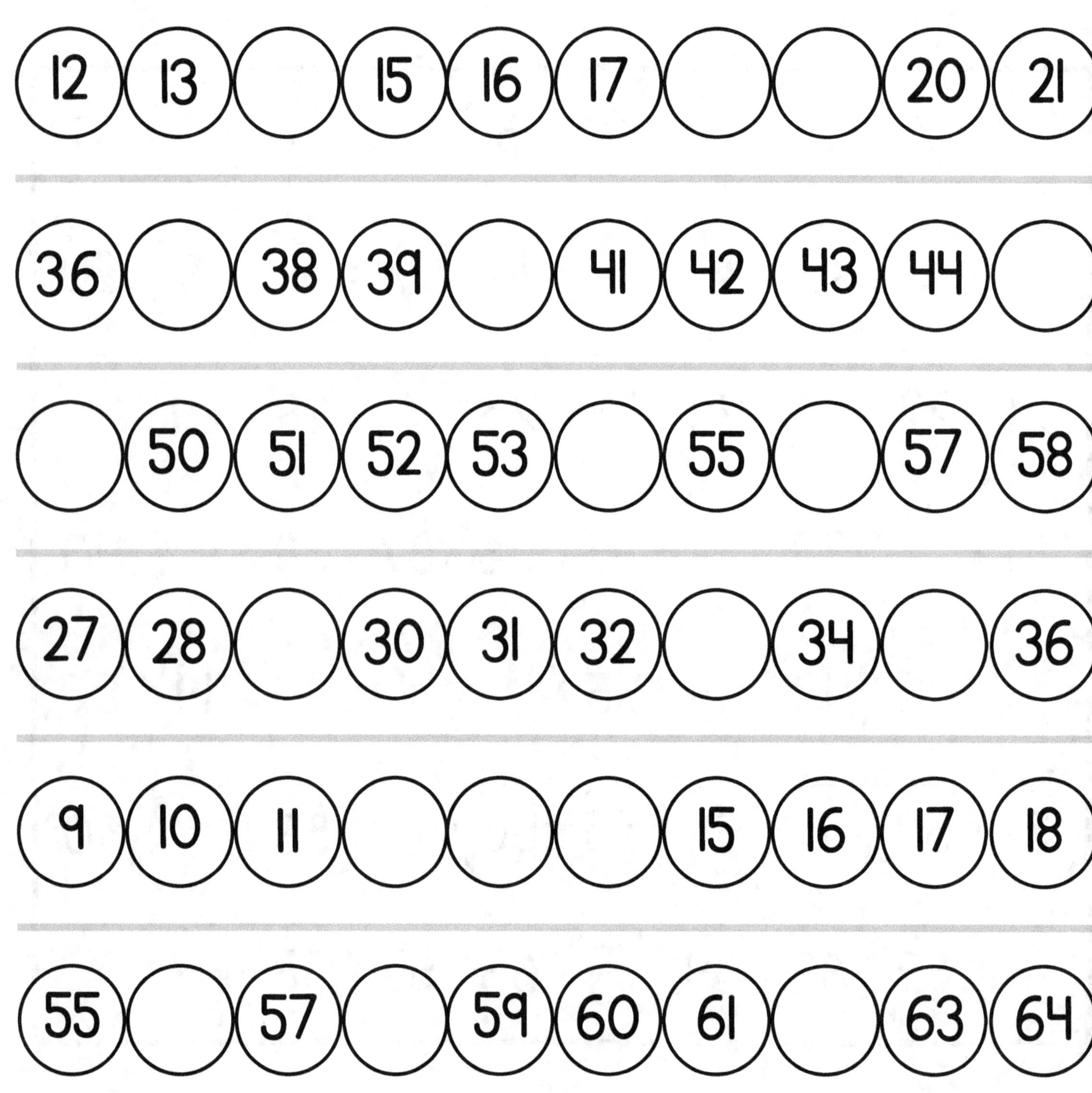

Color By Number 61-67

Connect the Dots 1-70

I Can Count to 80

1 2 3 4 5 6 7 8 9 10
11 12 13 14 15 16 17 18 19 20
21 22 23 24 25 26 27 28 29 30
31 32 33 34 35 36 37 38 39 40
41 42 43 44 45 46 47 48 49 50
51 52 53 54 55 56 57 58 59 60
61 62 63 64 65 66 67 68 69 70
71 72 73 74 75 76 77 78 79 80

I Can Write 1-80

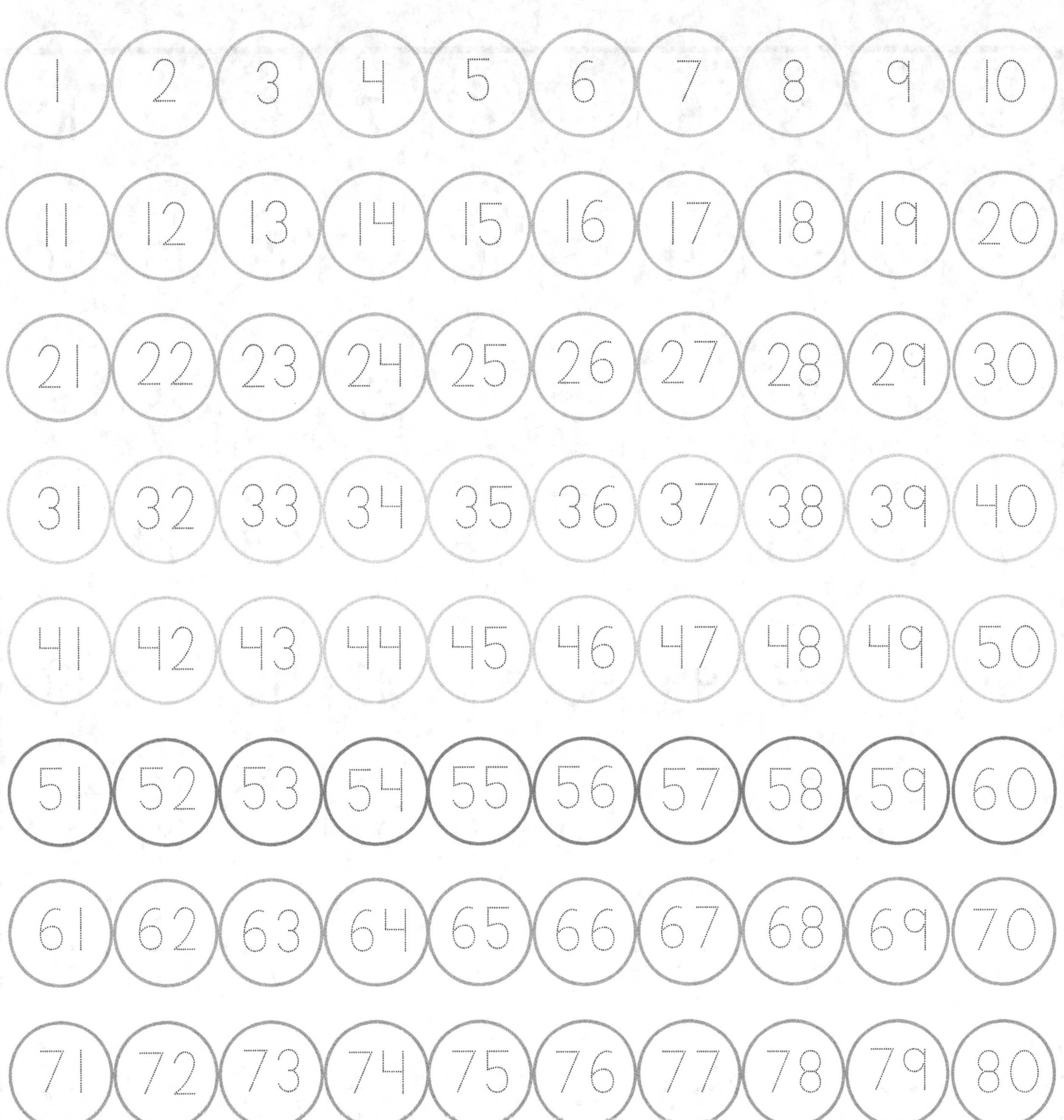

Write the missing numbers 1-80

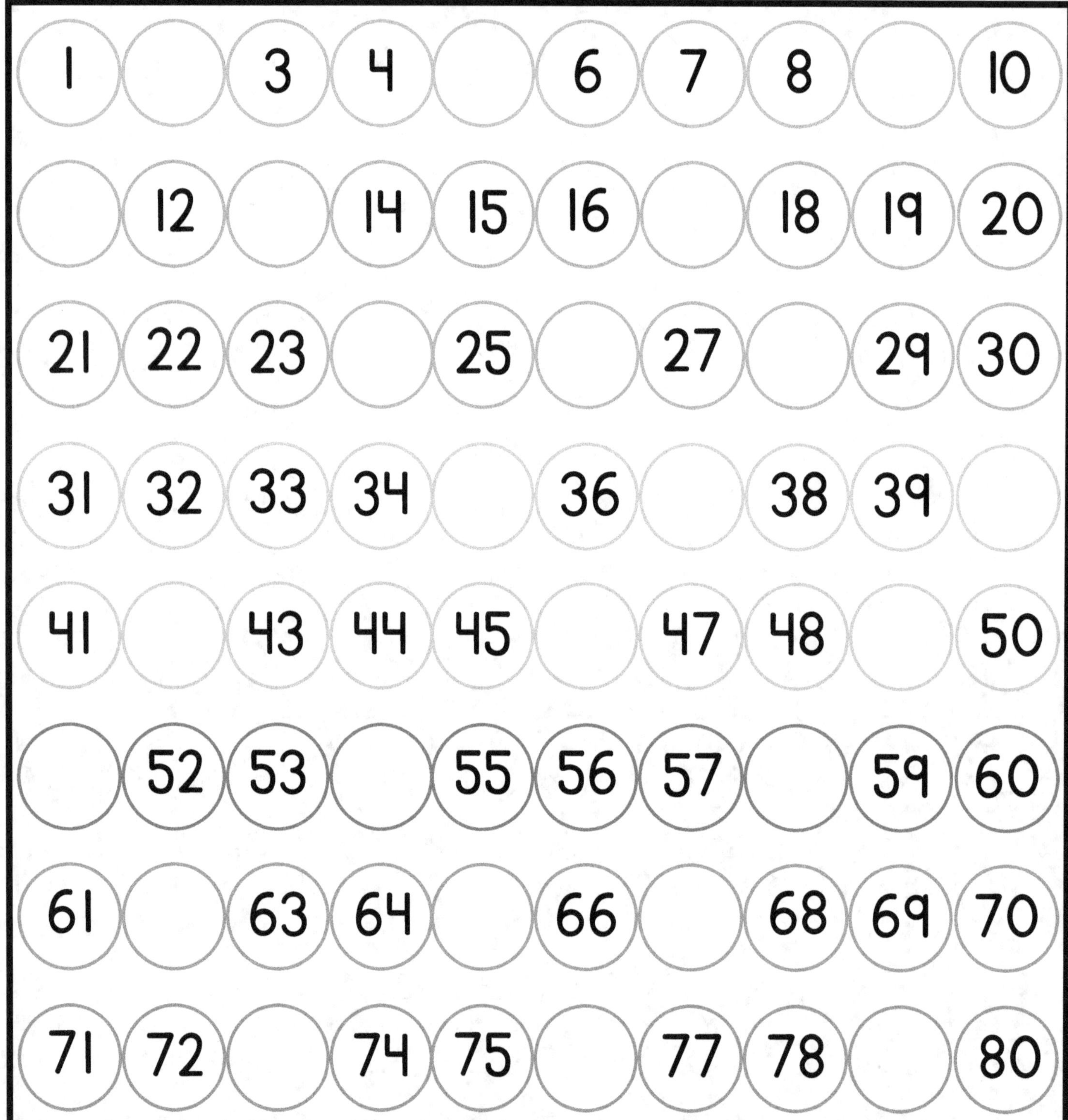

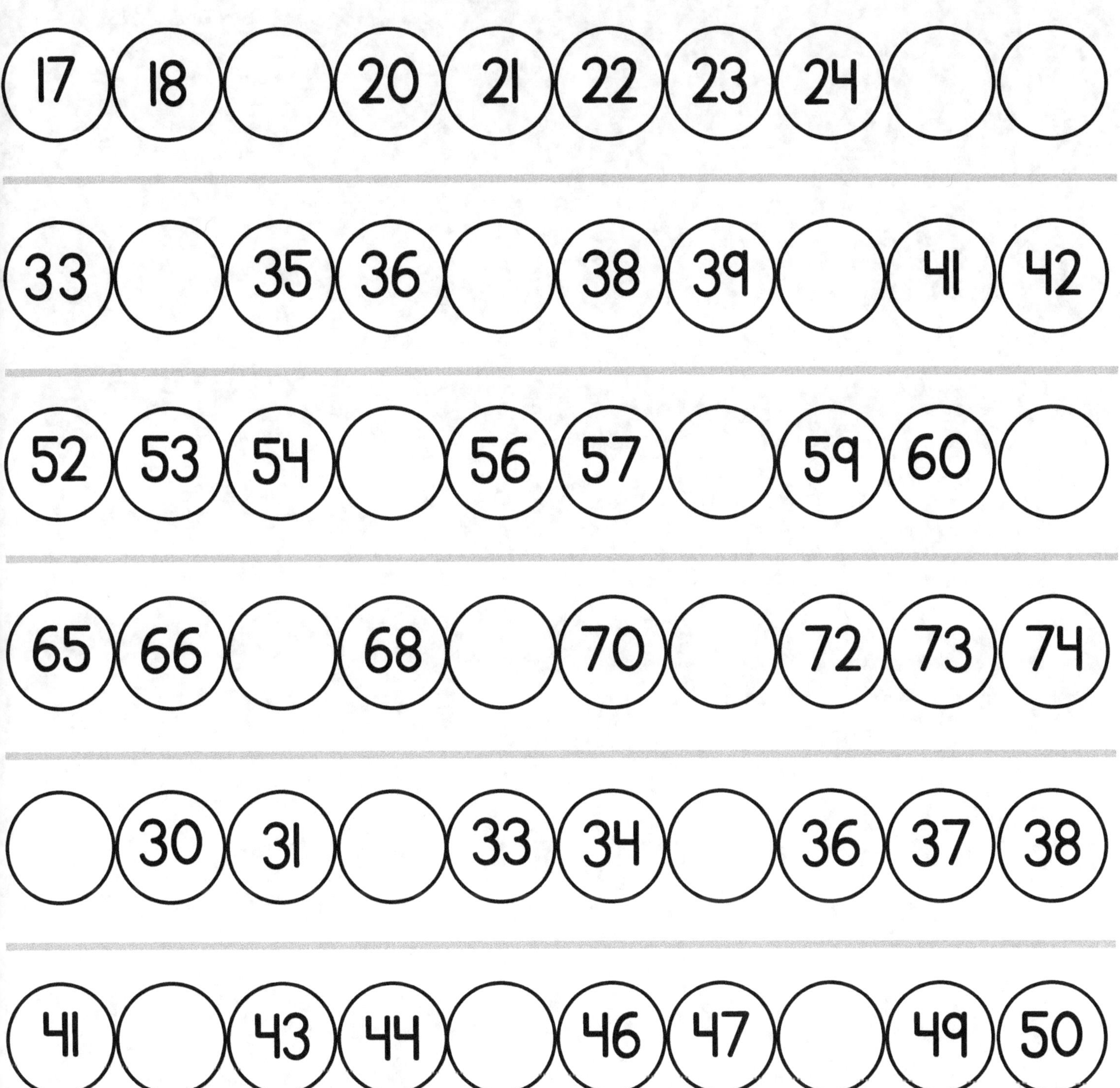

Write the missing numbers
1-80

Color By Number 71-77

71 light blue
72 purple
73 pink
74 yellow
75 brown
76 green
77 light brown

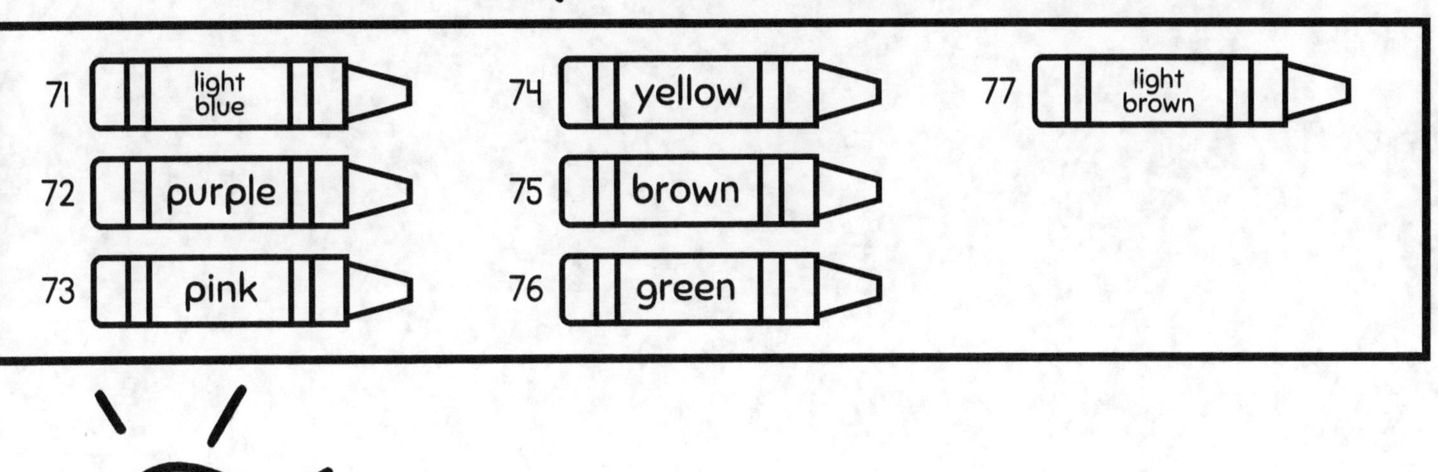

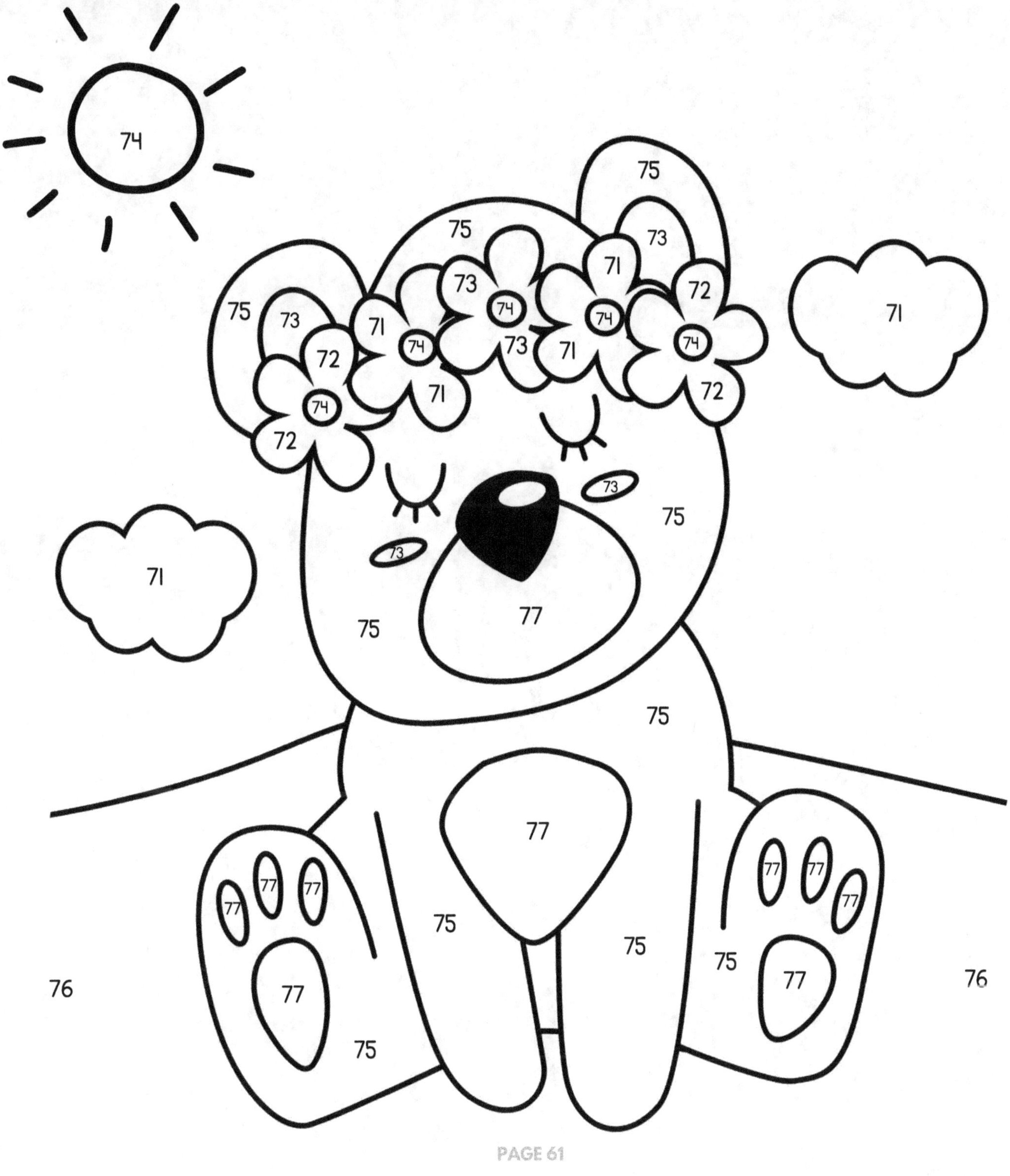

Connect the Dots 1-80

I Can Count to 90

1	2	3	4	5	6	7	8	9	10
11	12	13	14	15	16	17	18	19	20
21	22	23	24	25	26	27	28	29	30
31	32	33	34	35	36	37	38	39	40
41	42	43	44	45	46	47	48	49	50
51	52	53	54	55	56	57	58	59	60
61	62	63	64	65	66	67	68	69	70
71	72	73	74	75	76	77	78	79	80
81	82	83	84	85	86	87	88	89	90

I Can Write 1-90

1 2 3 4 5 6 7 8 9 10

11 12 13 14 15 16 17 18 19 20

21 22 23 24 25 26 27 28 29 30

31 32 33 34 35 36 37 38 39 40

41 42 43 44 45 46 47 48 49 50

51 52 53 54 55 56 57 58 59 60

61 62 63 64 65 66 67 68 69 70

71 72 73 74 75 76 77 78 79 80

81 82 83 84 85 86 87 88 89 90

Write the missing numbers 1-90

1	2	3		5	6	7	8		
11	12		14	15		17	18		20
	22	23	24		26	27	28	29	
31		33	34	35		37		39	40
41			44	45	46		48	49	50
	52	53		55	56	57	58		60
61	62	63		65	66		68		70
71		73	74	75		77		79	80
81	82		84		86		88	89	90

Write the missing numbers
1-90

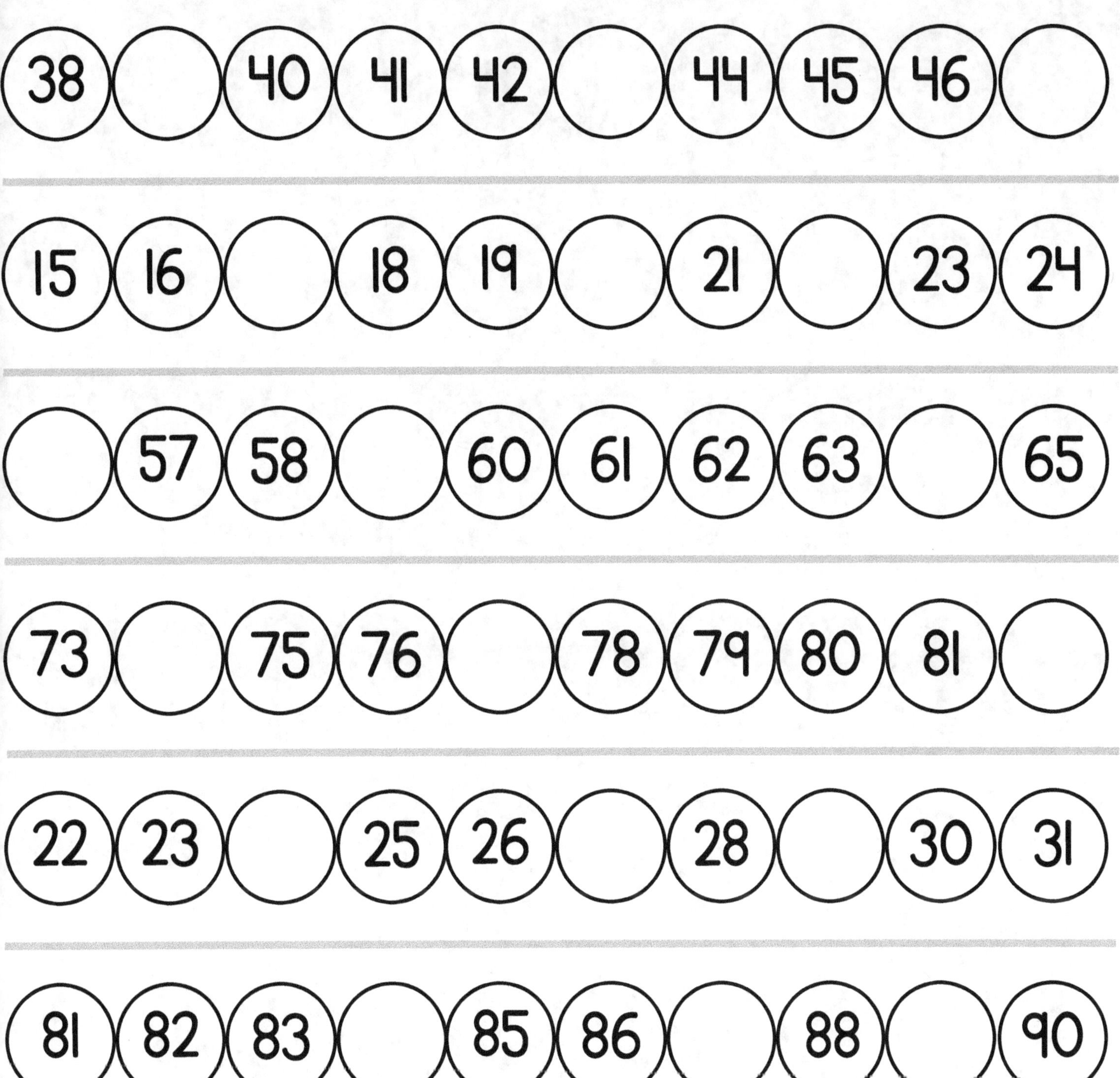

Color By Number 81-88

81	orange	84	yellow	87	black
82	green	85	blue	88	white
83	red	86	grey		

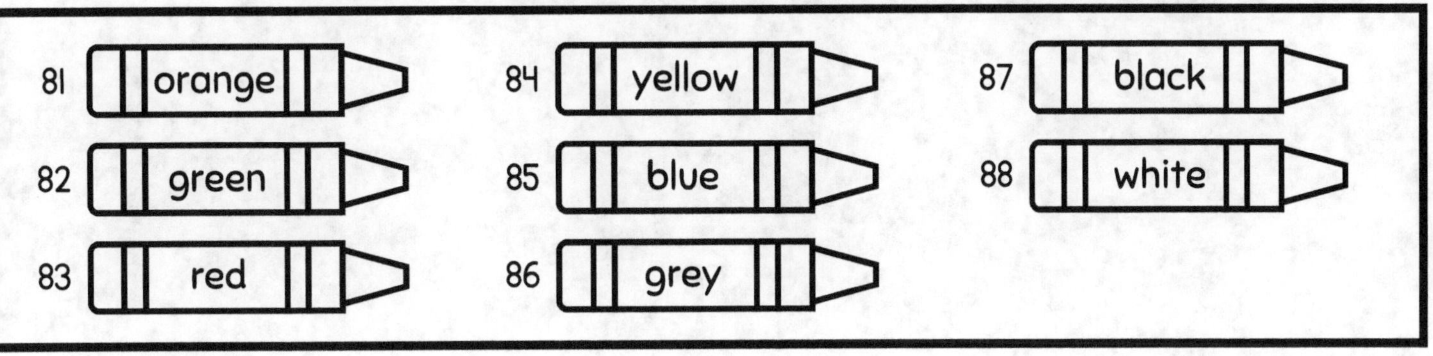

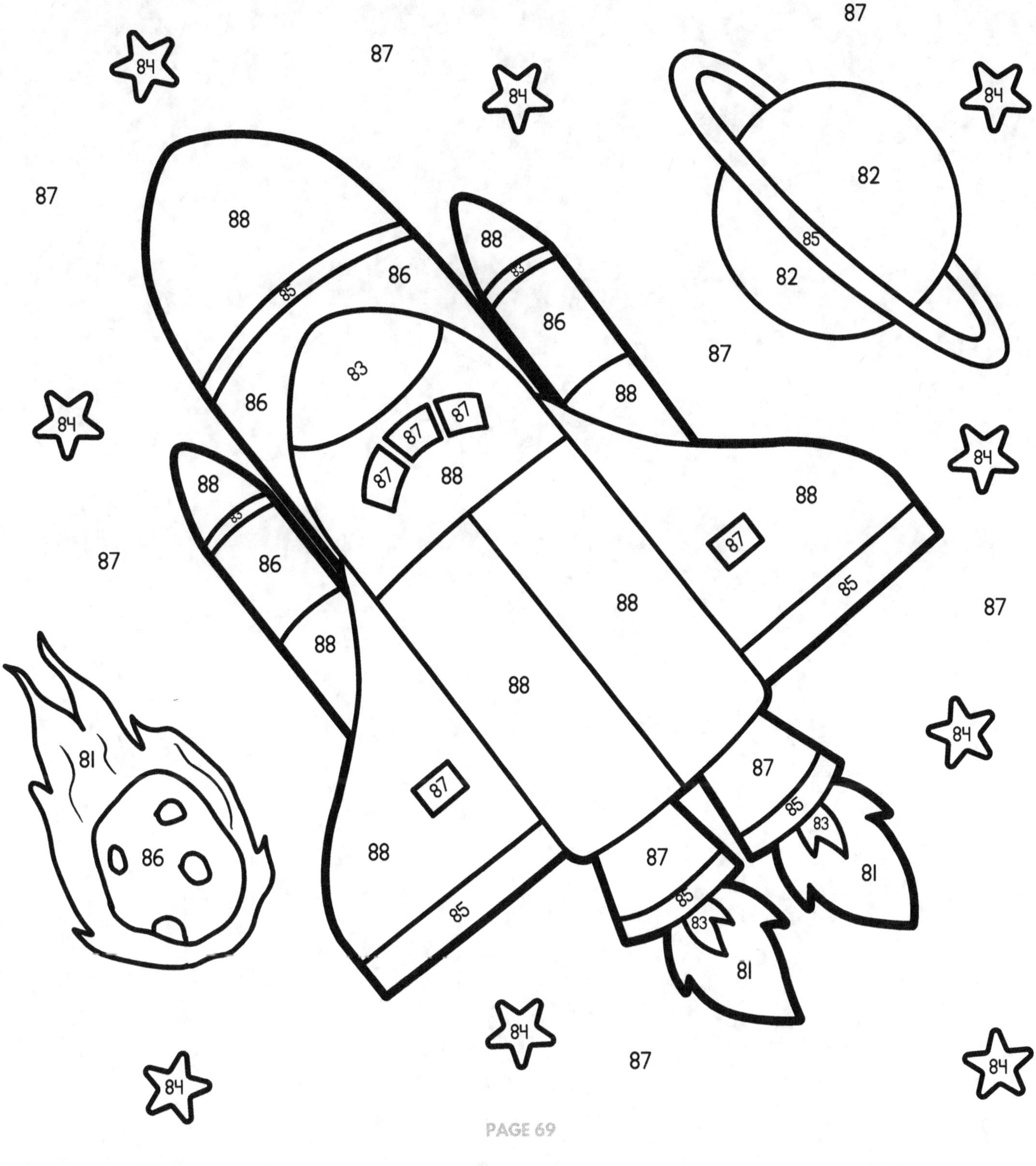

Connect the Dots 1-90

I Can Count to 100

1	2	3	4	5	6	7	8	9	10
11	12	13	14	15	16	17	18	19	20
21	22	23	24	25	26	27	28	29	30
31	32	33	34	35	36	37	38	39	40
41	42	43	44	45	46	47	48	49	50
51	52	53	54	55	56	57	58	59	60
61	62	63	64	65	66	67	68	69	70
71	72	73	74	75	76	77	78	79	80
81	82	83	84	85	86	87	88	89	90
91	92	93	94	95	96	97	98	99	100

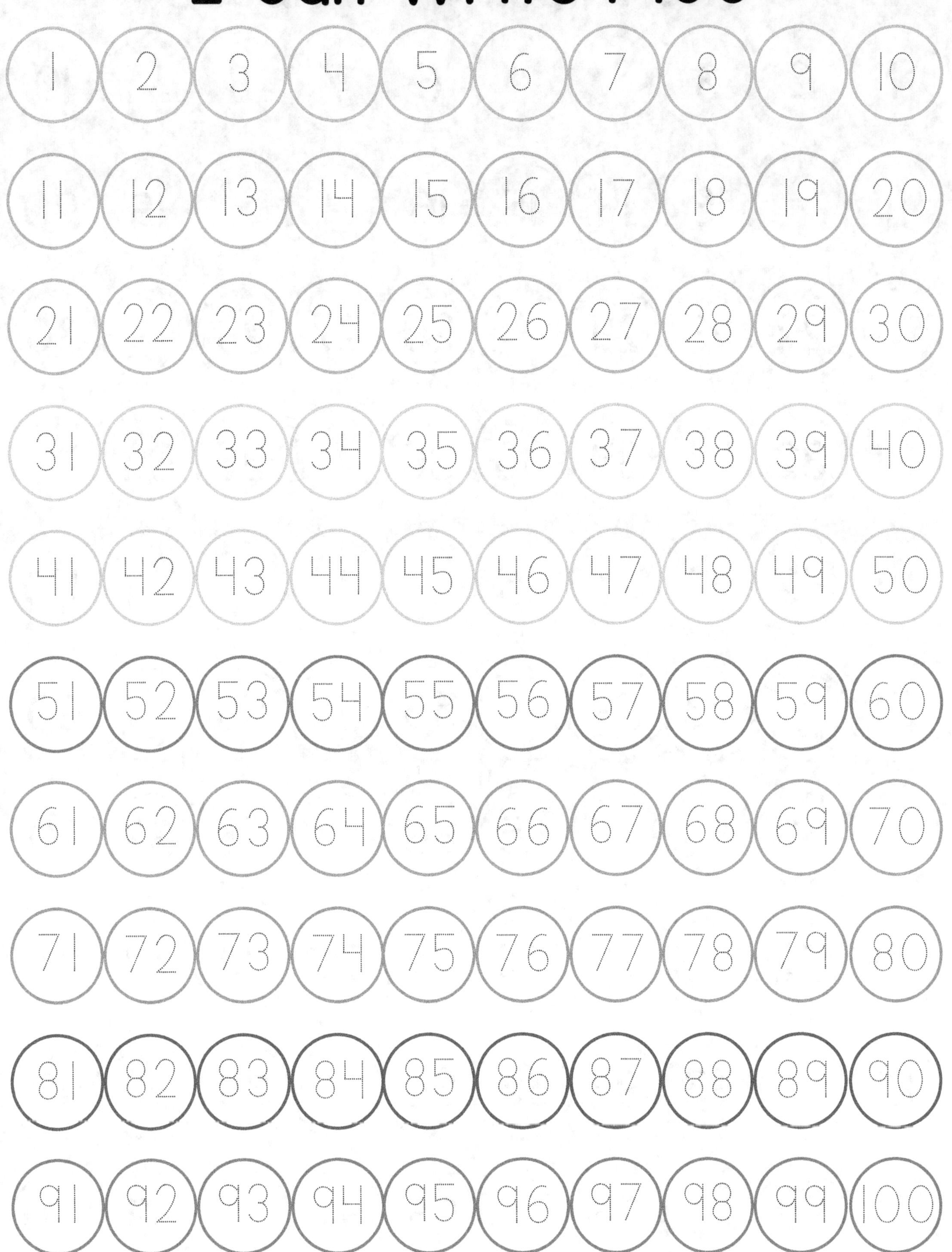

I Can Write 1-100
1 2 3 4 5 6 7 8 9 10
11 12 13 14 15 16 17 18 19 20
21 22 23 24 25 26 27 28 29 30
31 32 33 34 35 36 37 38 39 40
41 42 43 44 45 46 47 48 49 50
51 52 53 54 55 56 57 58 59 60
61 62 63 64 65 66 67 68 69 70
71 72 73 74 75 76 77 78 79 80
81 82 83 84 85 86 87 88 89 90
91 92 93 94 95 96 97 98 99 100

Write the missing numbers 1-100

1	2	3			6	7	8		10
11		13	14	15	16			19	20
	22	23	24		26	27	28		30
31	32		34	35	36		38	39	
41	42	43		45		47		49	50
51		53	54		56	57	58		60
	62	63		65	66		68	69	70
71	72		74	75		77	78	79	
81		83	84	85	86		88		90
91	92		94		96	97		99	100

Write the missing numbers 1-100

1			4	5	6	7	8	9	
11	12		14	15	16		18		20
21	22	23	24			27		29	30
	32	33		35	36	37	38		40
41		43	44	45	46		48	49	
51	52		54		56	57		59	60
61	62	63		65		67	68		70
	72	73	74	75	76		78	79	
81		83	84		86	87		89	90
91	92		94	95		97	98		100

Write the missing numbers 1-100

11	12	13	14	15	16	17	18	19	20
31	32	33	34	35	36	37	38	39	40
51	52	53	54	55	56	57	58	59	60
71	72	73	74	75	76	77	78	79	80
91	92	93	94	95	96	97	98	99	100

Write the missing numbers 1-100

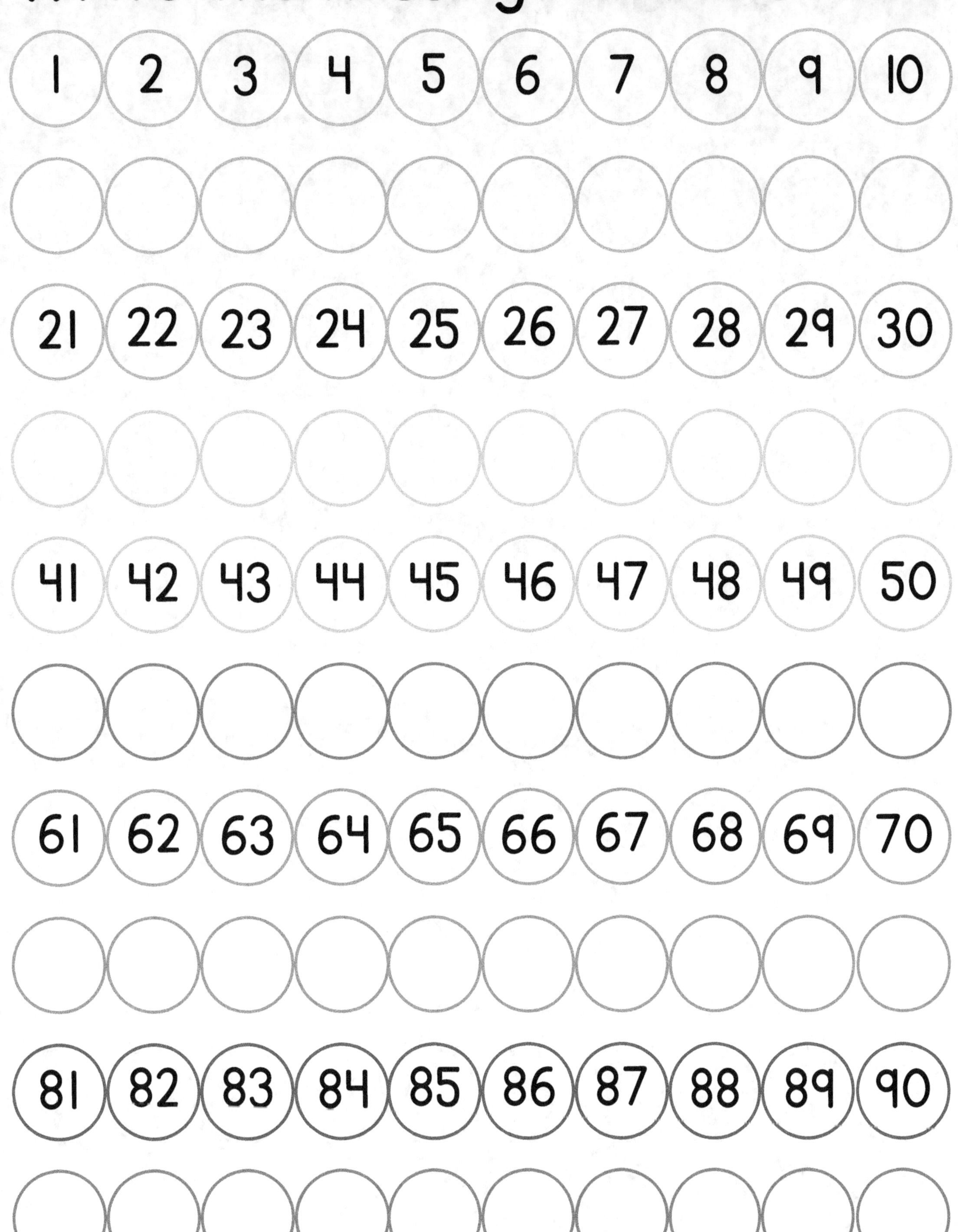

I Can Write 1-100

I Can Write 1-100

Write the missing numbers 1-100

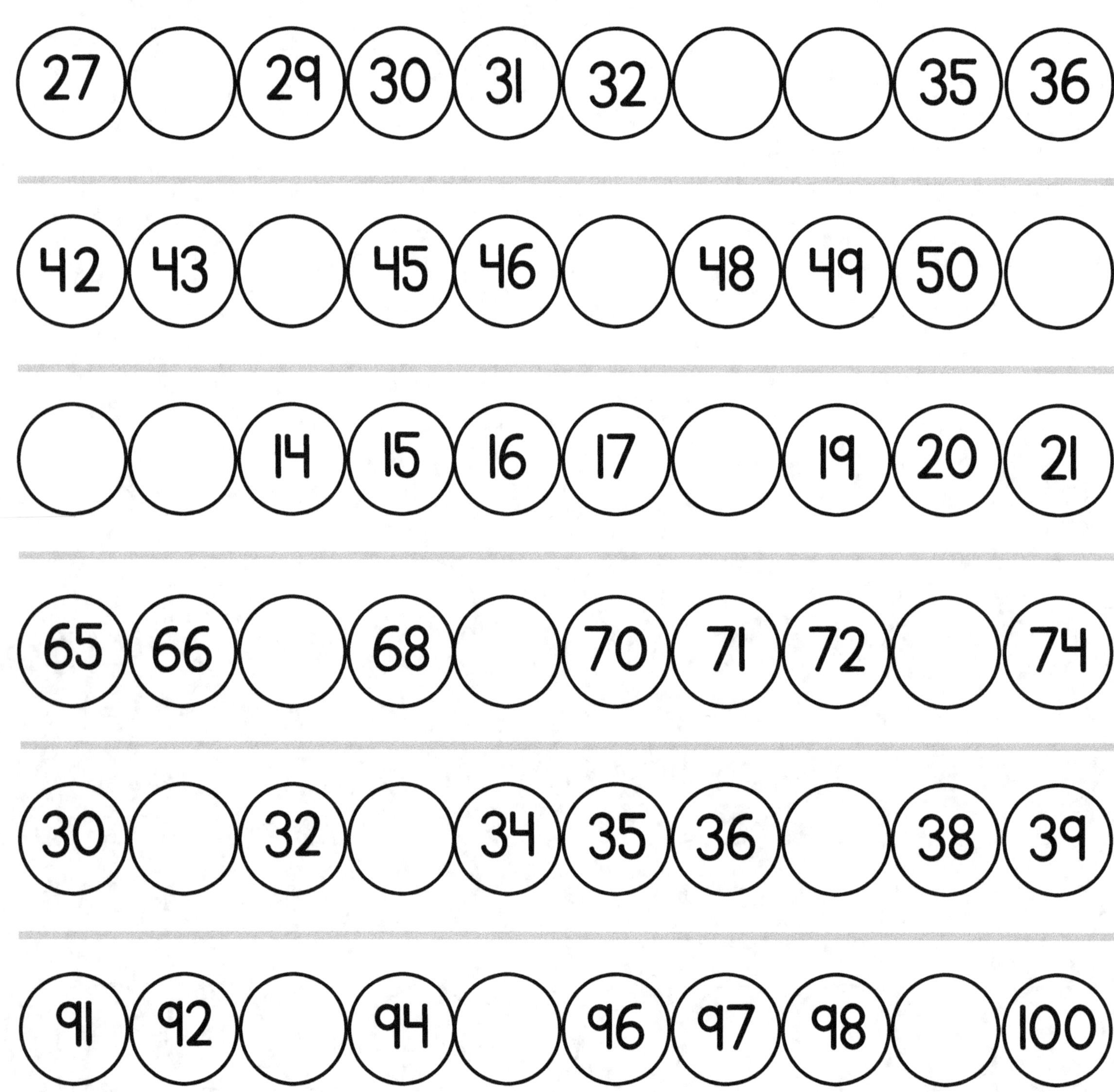

Write the missing numbers 1-100

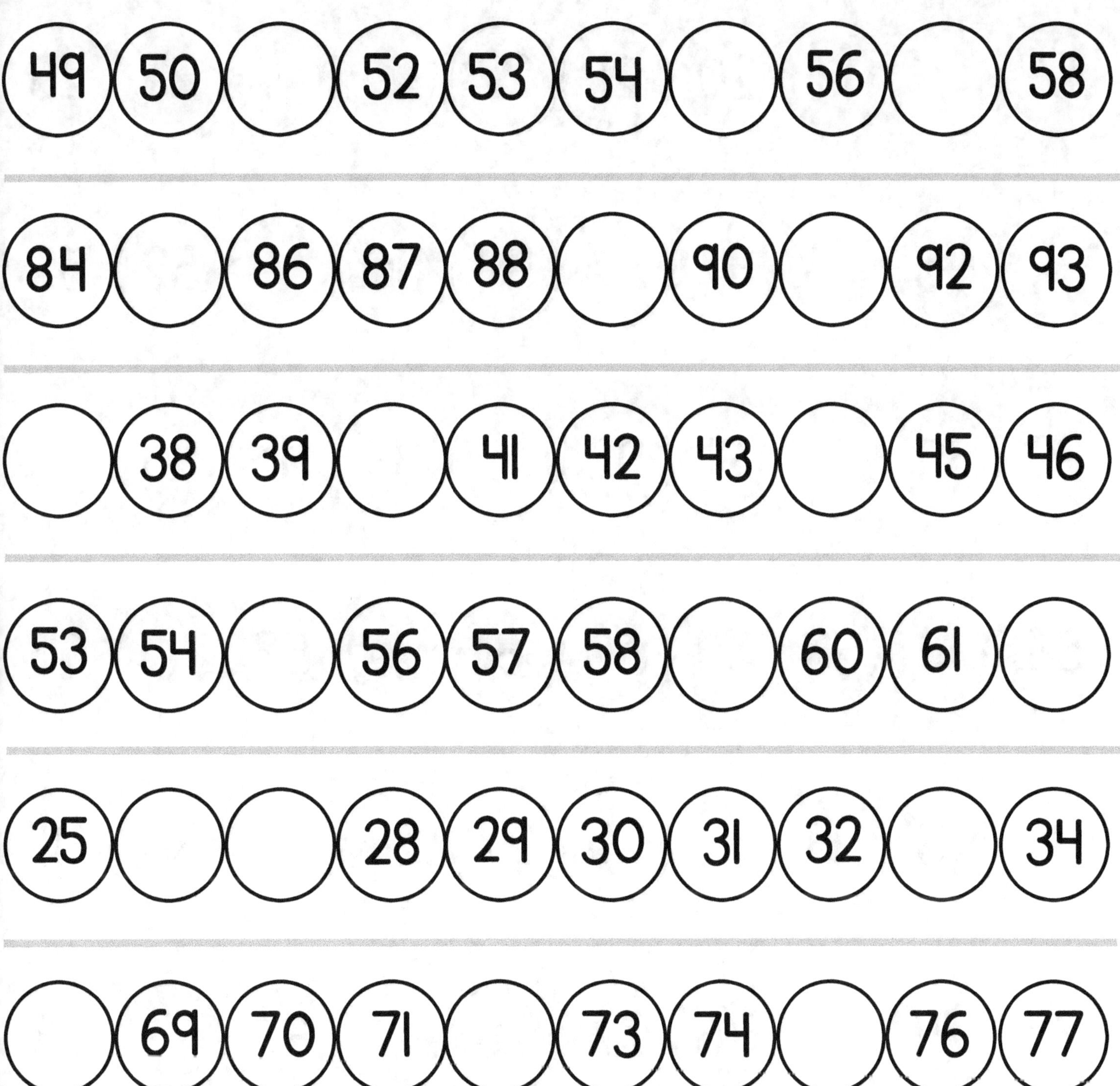

Write the missing numbers
1-100

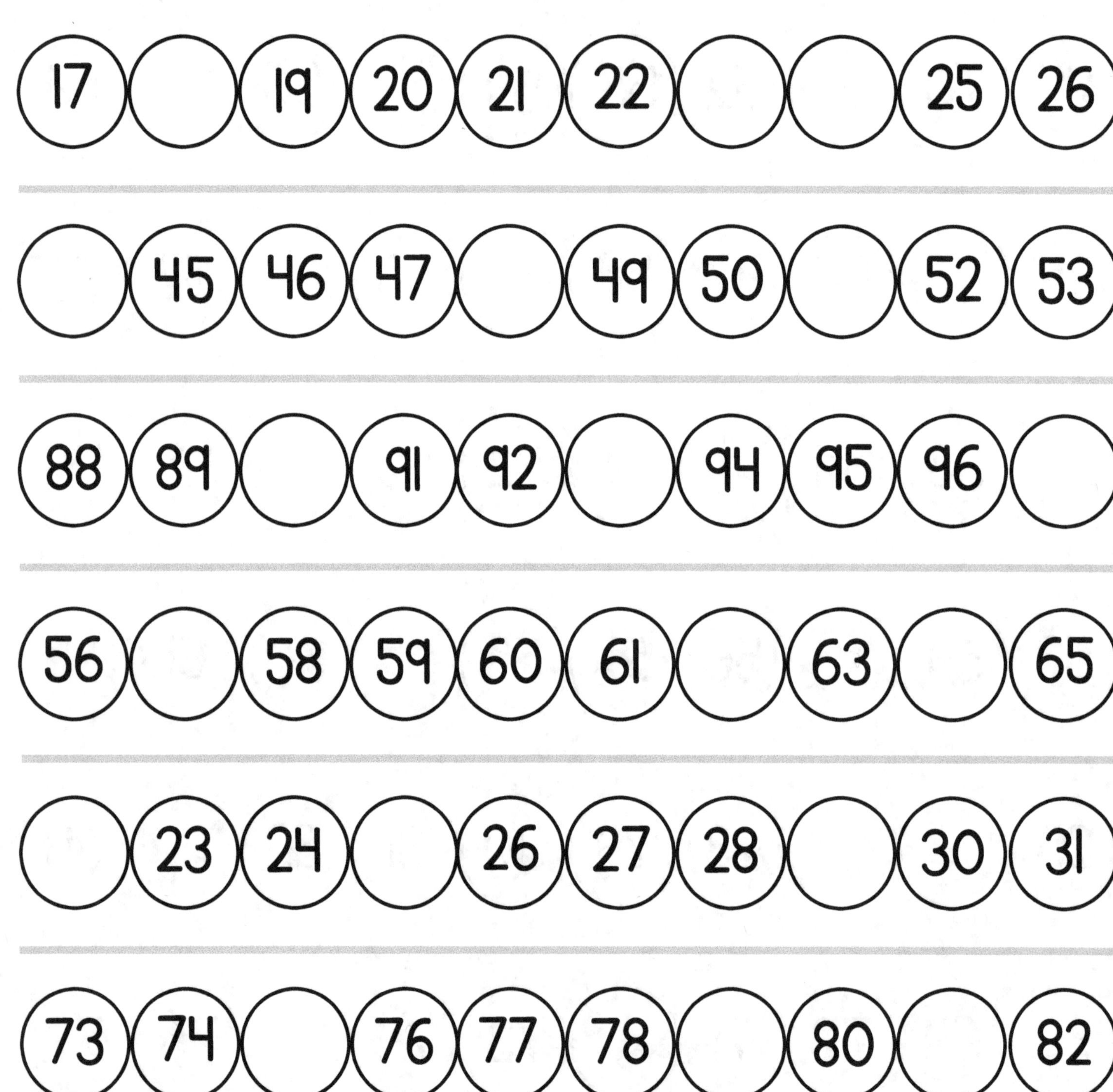

Color By Number 91-98

91 light green	94 dark green	97 light blue
92 orange	95 pink	98 purple
93 blue	96 black	

Connect the Dots 1-100

Bonus Section!

Learn to Skip Count

After they can count to 100 kids can learn to skip count!

In this book we'll cover skip counting by 10's & 5's.

Skip Counting by 10's

Follow the arrows to count to 100 by 10's

1	2	3	4	5	6	7	8	9	10
11	12	13	14	15	16	17	18	19	20
21	22	23	24	25	26	27	28	29	30
31	32	33	34	35	36	37	38	39	40
41	42	43	44	45	46	47	48	49	50
51	52	53	54	55	56	57	58	59	60
61	62	63	64	65	66	67	68	69	70
71	72	73	74	75	76	77	78	79	80
81	82	83	84	85	86	87	88	89	90
91	92	93	94	95	96	97	98	99	100

Practice Skip Counting by 10's

Practice Skip Counting by counting groups of 10.

(Get hands on by using counting cubes, coins, marbles, goldfish, any small items
hat you can easily sort into groups of 10.)

Practice Skip Counting by 10's

Practice Skip Counting by counting groups of 10.

(Get hands on by using counting cubes, coins, marbles, goldfish, any small items
hat you can easily sort into groups of 10.)

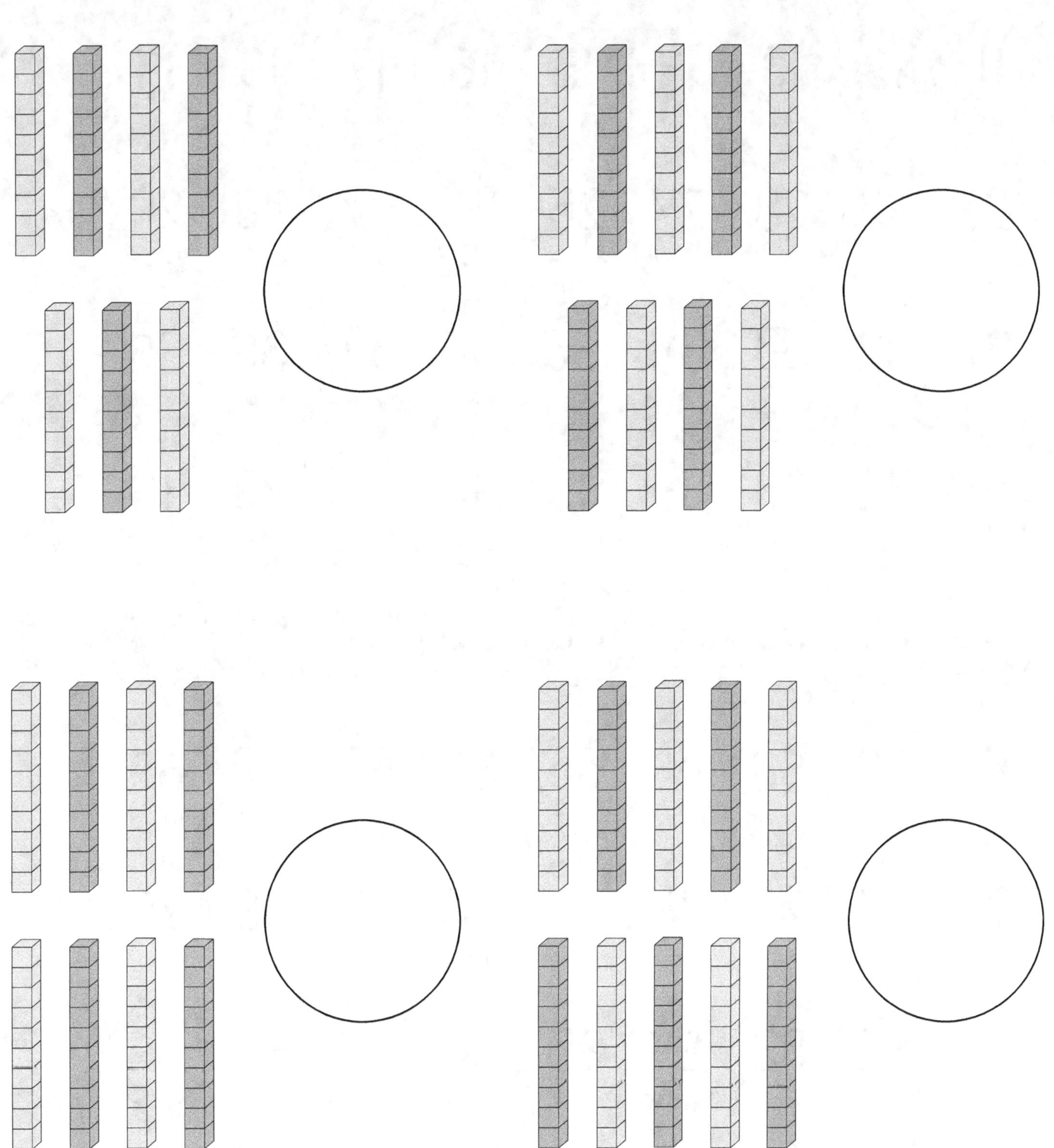

Skip Counting by 10's

Practice by tracing the numbers to count by 10s

1	2	3	4	5	6	7	8	9	10
11	12	13	14	15	16	17	18	19	20
21	22	23	24	25	26	27	28	29	30
31	32	33	34	35	36	37	38	39	40
41	42	43	44	45	46	47	48	49	50
51	52	53	54	55	56	57	58	59	60
61	62	63	64	65	66	67	68	69	70
71	72	73	74	75	76	77	78	79	80
81	82	83	84	85	86	87	88	89	90
91	92	93	94	95	96	97	98	99	100

Write the missing numbers
to count to 100 by 10's

1	2	3	4	5	6	7	8	9	
11	12	13	14	15	16	17	18	19	
21	22	23	24	25	26	27	28	29	
31	32	33	34	35	36	37	38	39	
41	42	43	44	45	46	47	48	49	
51	52	53	54	55	56	57	58	59	
61	62	63	64	65	66	67	68	69	
71	72	73	74	75	76	77	78	79	
81	82	83	84	85	86	87	88	89	
91	92	93	94	95	96	97	98	99	

Write the missing numbers
Skip Counting by 10's

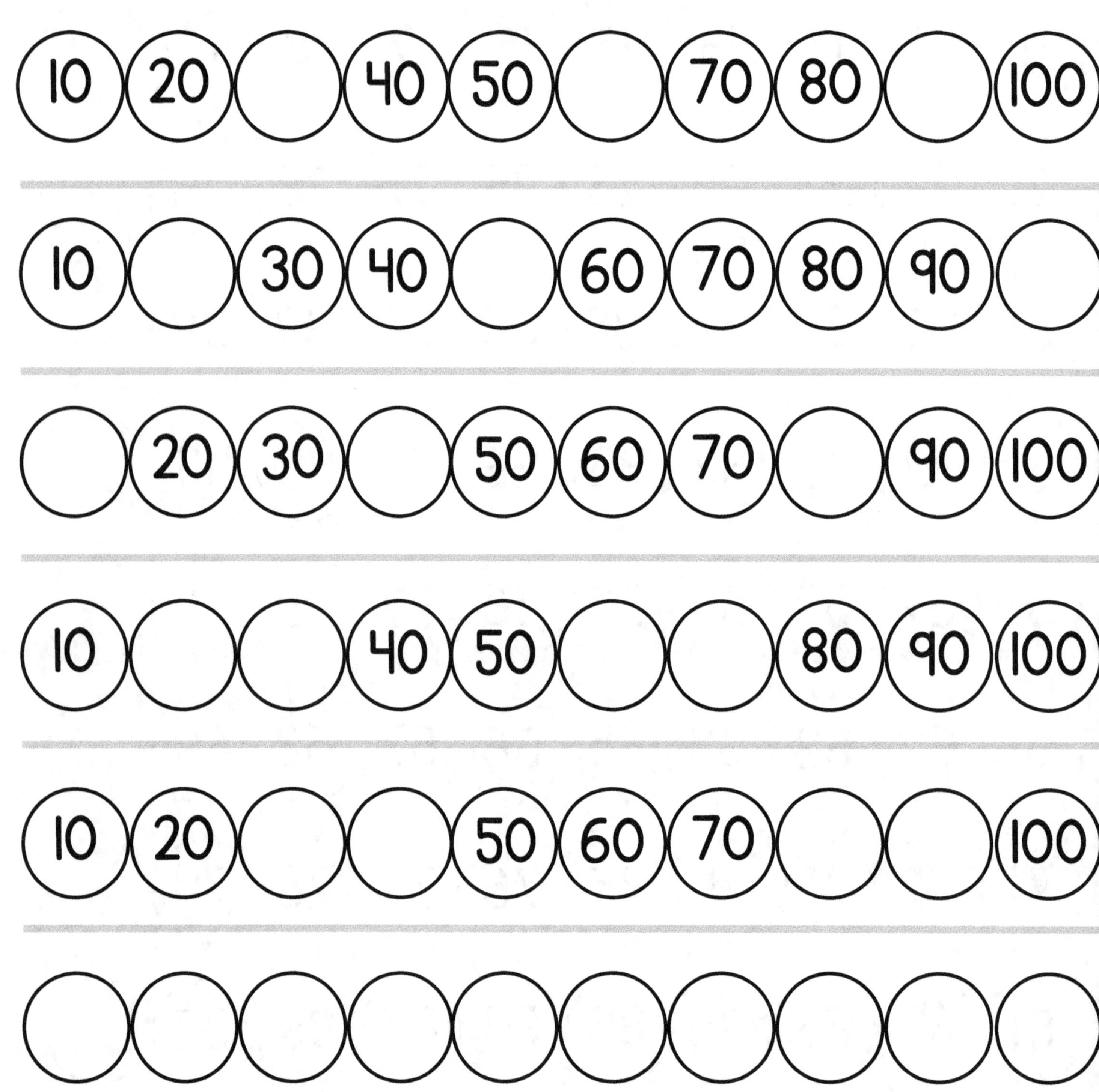

Skip Counting by 5's

Follow the arrows to count to 100 by 5's

(Parents you may want to highlight the correct numbers.)

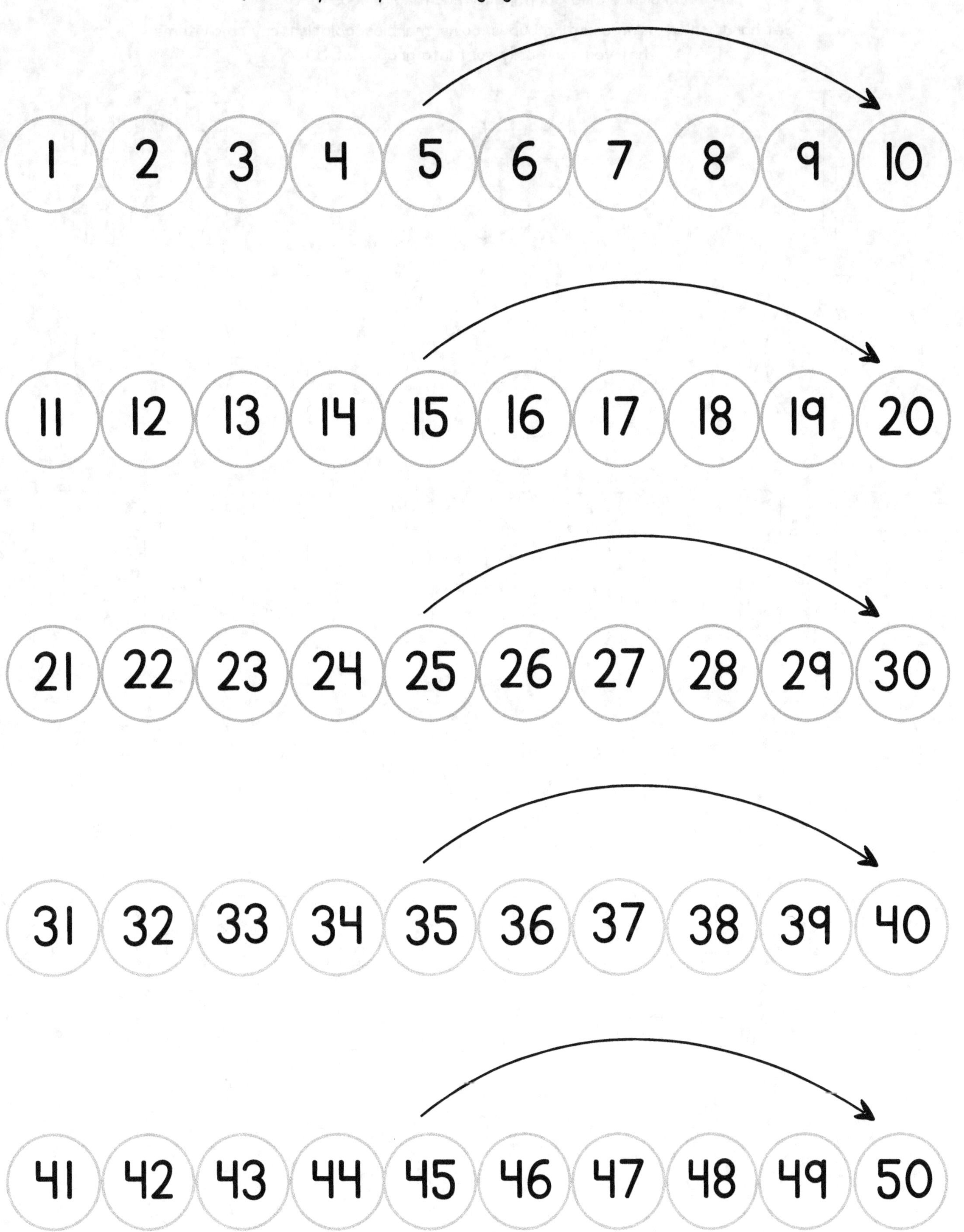

Practice Skip Counting by 5's

Practice Skip Counting by counting groups of 5.
(Get hands on by using counting cubes, coins, marbles, goldfish, any small items
hat you can easily sort into groups of 5.)

Practice Skip Counting by 5's

Practice Skip Counting by counting groups of 5.

(Get hands on by using counting cubes, coins, marbles, goldfish, any small items
hat you can easily sort into groups of 5.)

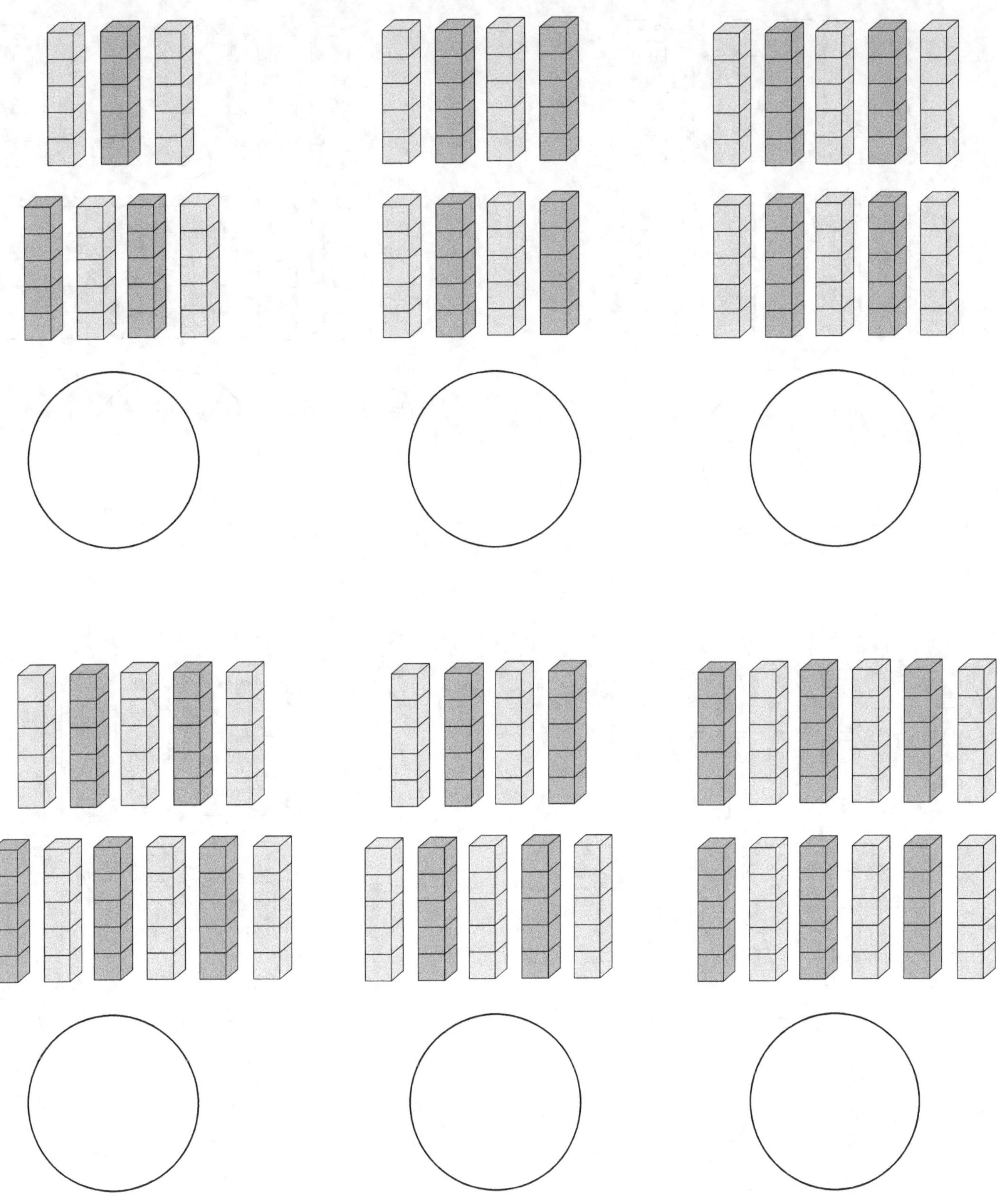

Practice Skip Counting by 5's

Practice Skip Counting by counting groups of 5.

(Get hands on by using counting cubes, coins, marbles, goldfish, any small items
hat you can easily sort into groups of 5.)

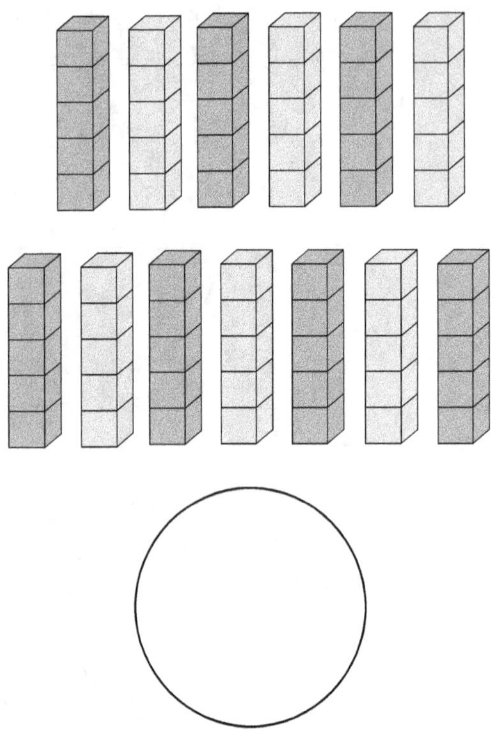

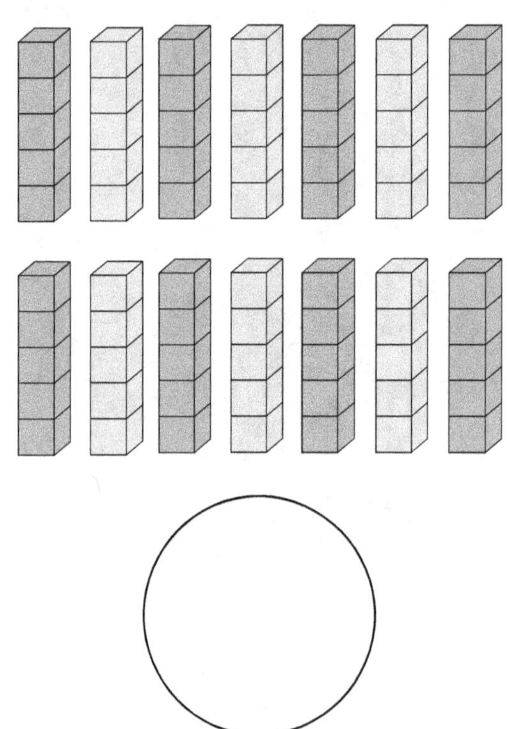

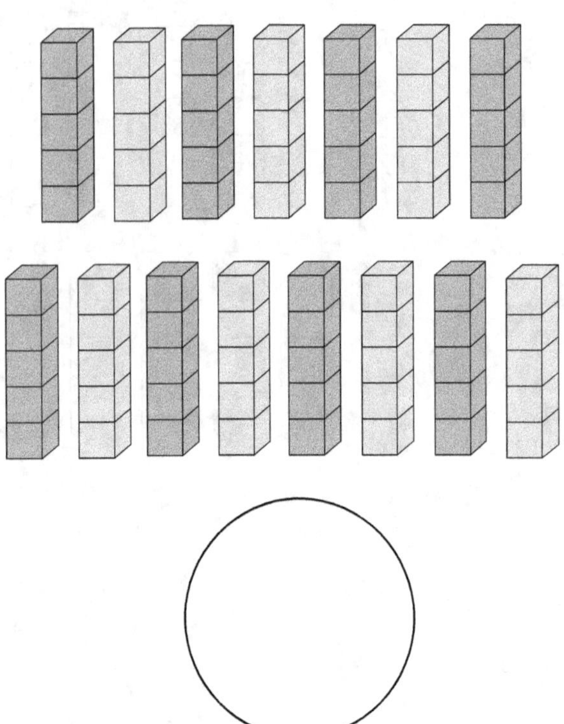

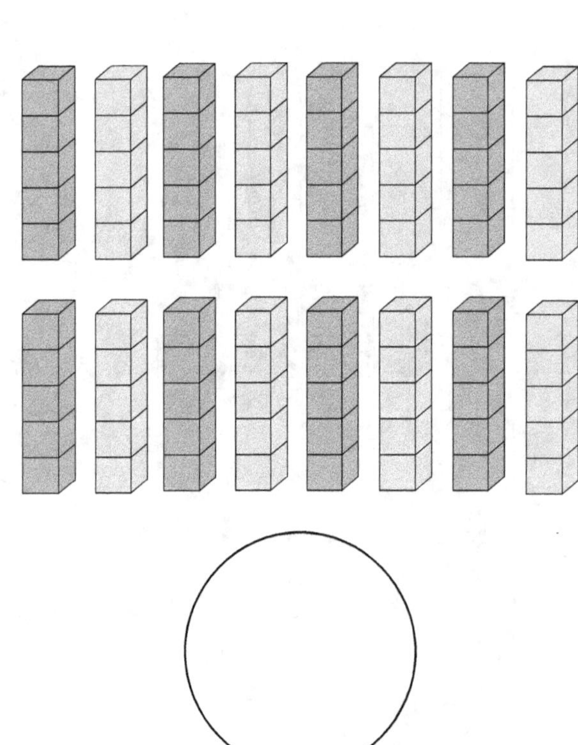

Practice Skip Counting by 5's

Practice Skip Counting by counting groups of 5.

(Get hands on by using counting cubes, coins, marbles, goldfish, any small items
hat you can easily sort into groups of 5.)

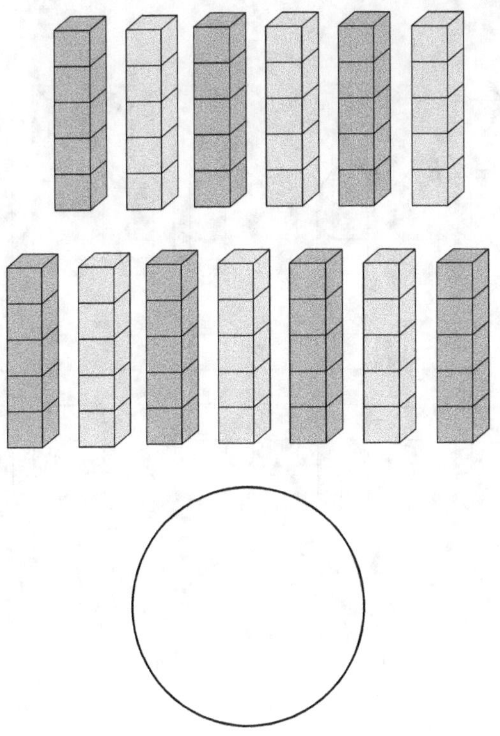

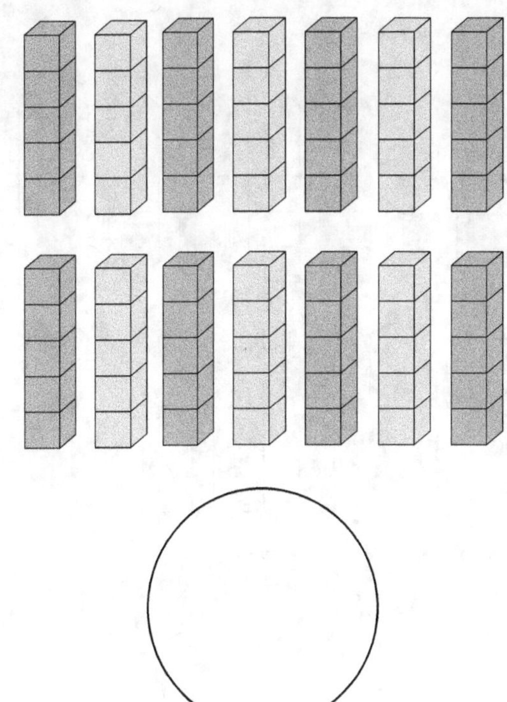

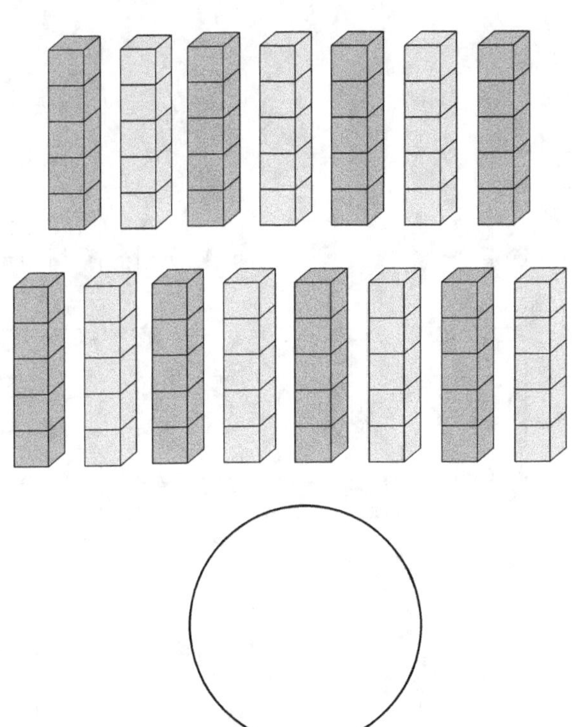

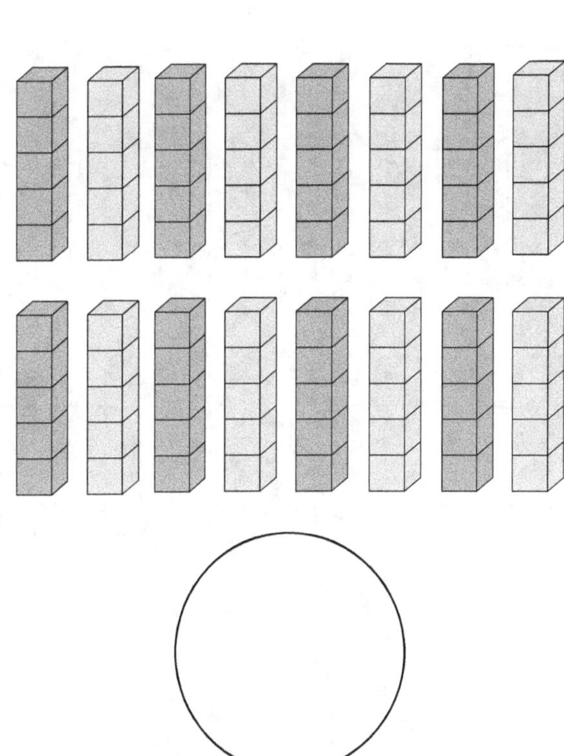

Practice Skip Counting by 5's

Practice Skip Counting by counting groups of 5.

(Get hands on by using counting cubes, coins, marbles, goldfish, any small items
hat you can easily sort into groups of 5.)

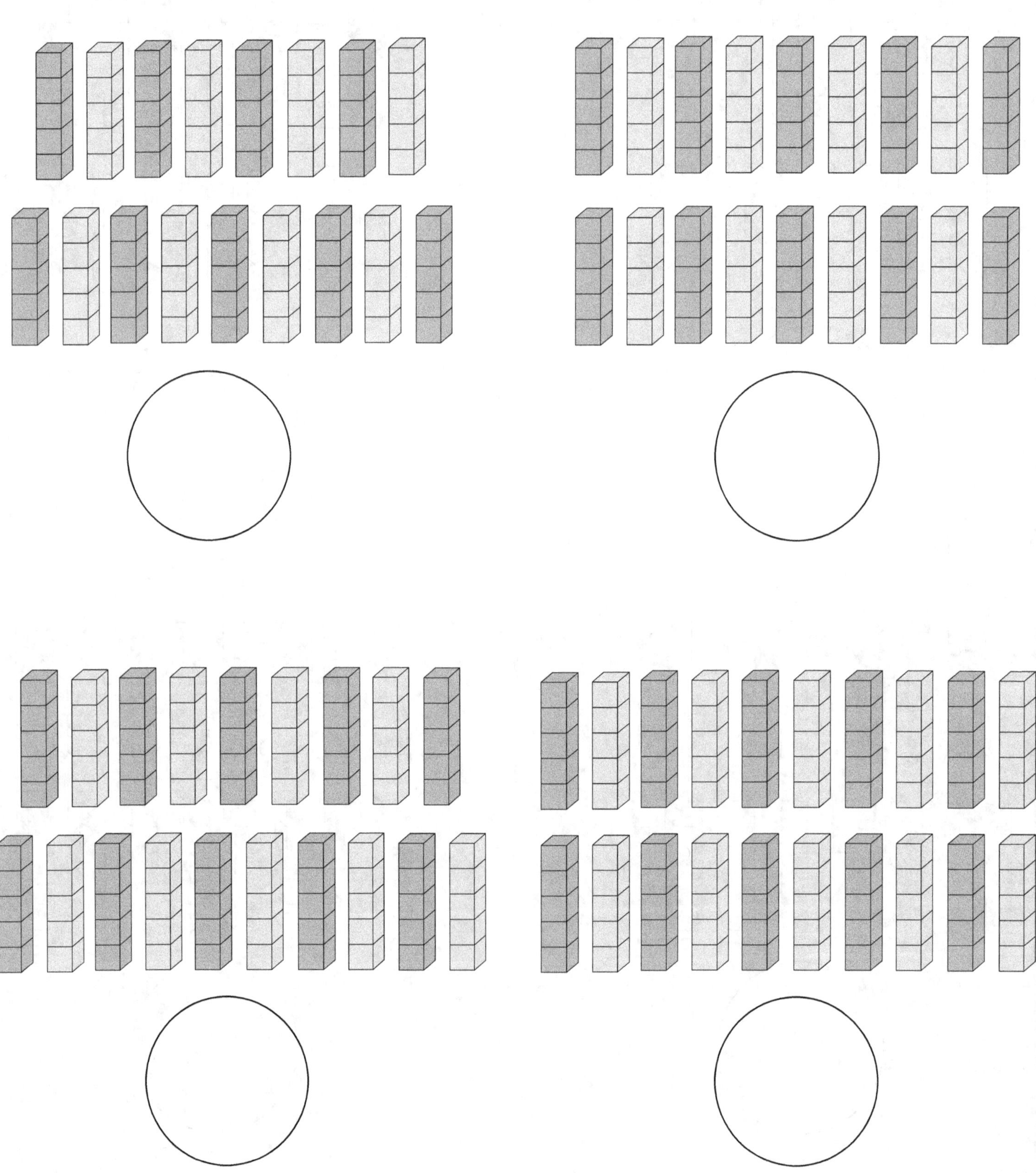

Skip Counting by 5's

Practice by tracing the numbers to count by 5's

1	2	3	4	5	6	7	8	9	10
11	12	13	14	15	16	17	18	19	20
21	22	23	24	25	26	27	28	29	30
31	32	33	34	35	36	37	38	39	40
41	42	43	44	45	46	47	48	49	50
51	52	53	54	55	56	57	58	59	60
61	62	63	64	65	66	67	68	69	70
71	72	73	74	75	76	77	78	79	80
81	82	83	84	85	86	87	88	89	90
91	92	93	94	95	96	97	98	99	100

Write the missing numbers to count to 100 by 5's

1	2	3	4		6	7	8	9	
11	12	13	14		16	17	18	19	
21	22	23	24		26	27	28	29	
31	32	33	34		36	37	38	39	
41	42	43	44		46	47	48	49	
51	52	53	54		56	57	58	59	
61	62	63	64		66	67	68	69	
71	72	73	74		76	77	78	79	
81	82	83	84		86	87	88	89	
91	92	93	94		96	97	98	99	

Write the missing numbers
Skip Counting by 5's

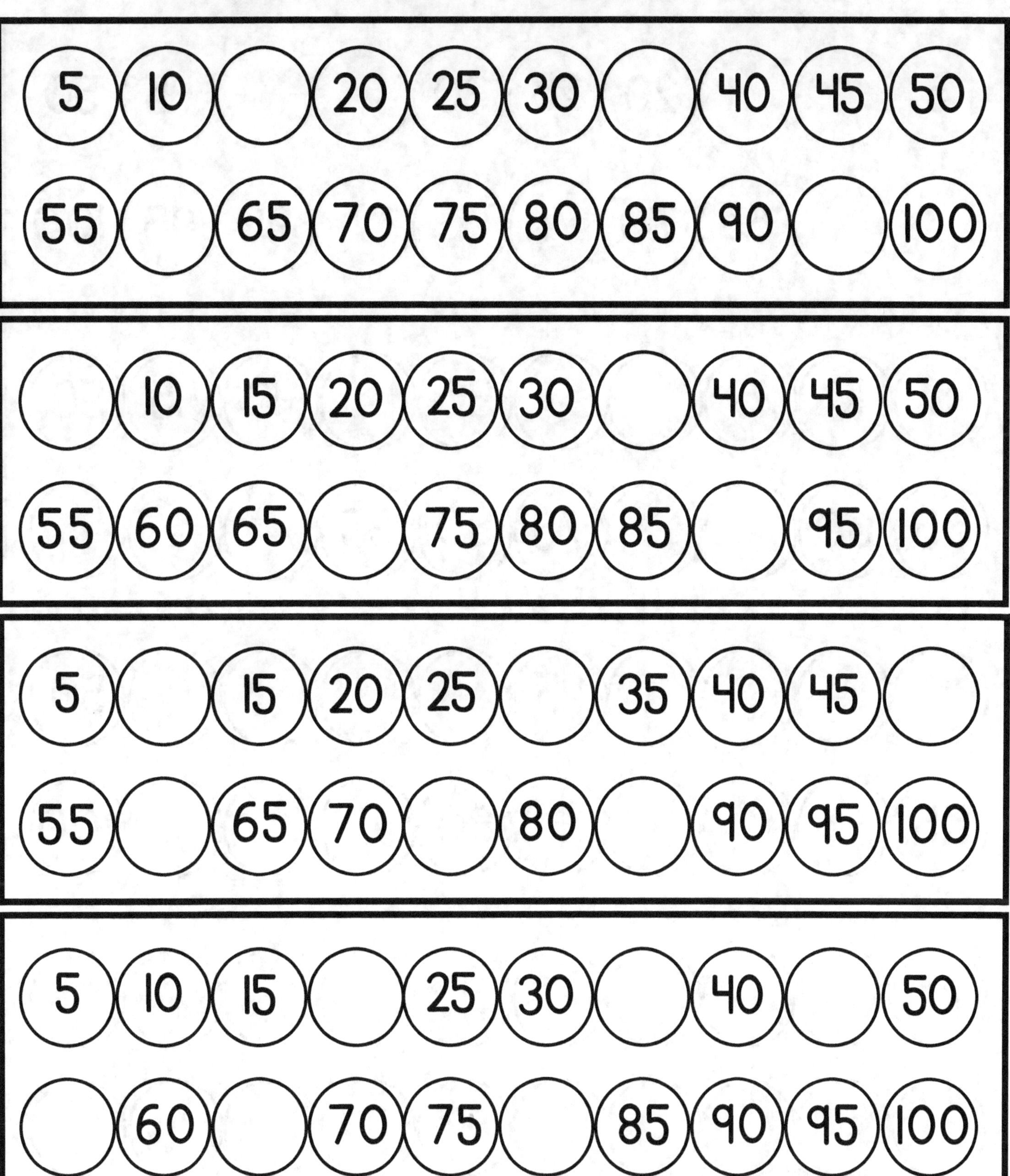

Write the missing numbers
Skip Counting by 5's

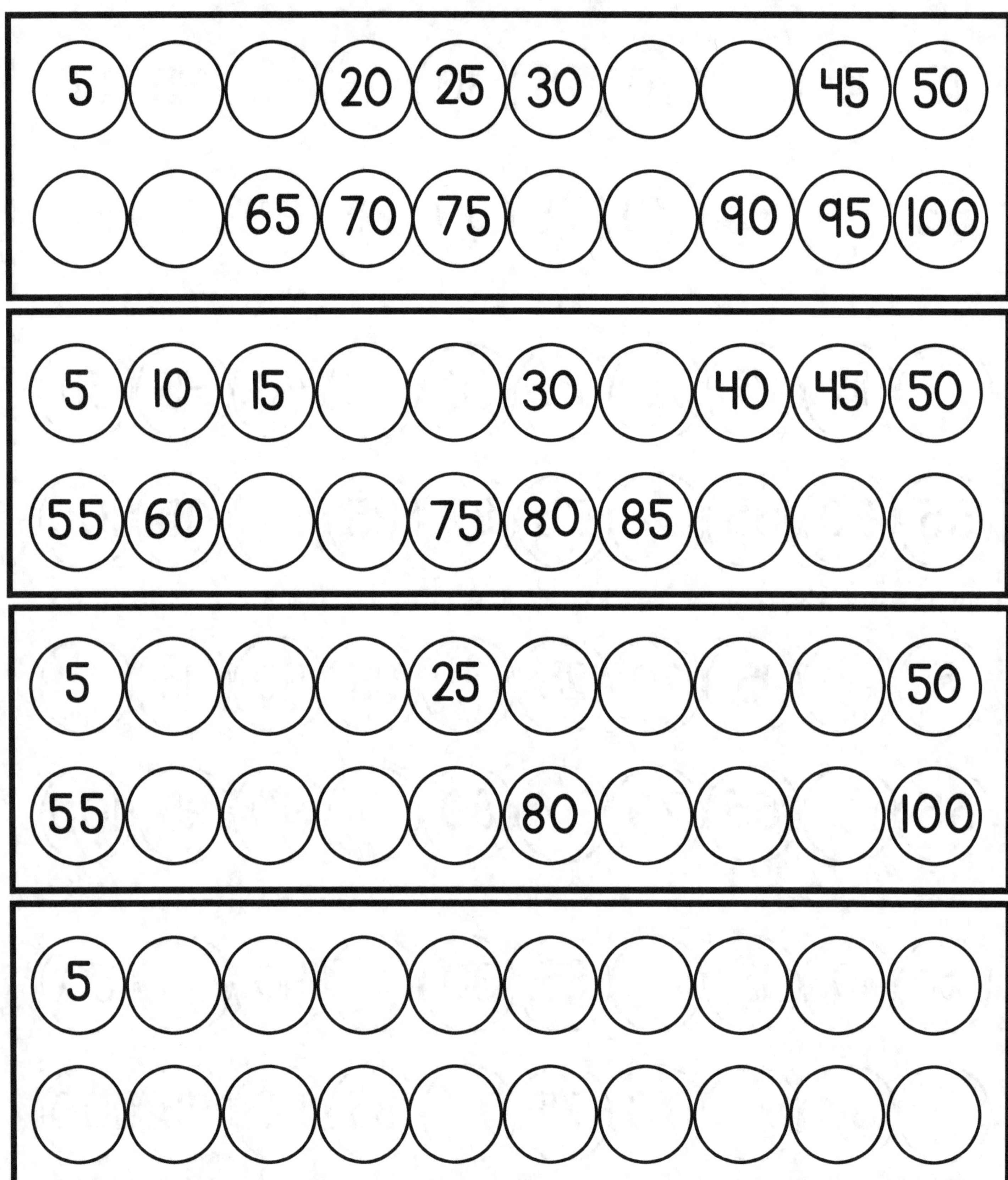